SEARCH ON SINAI

SHILOH ON SINAI

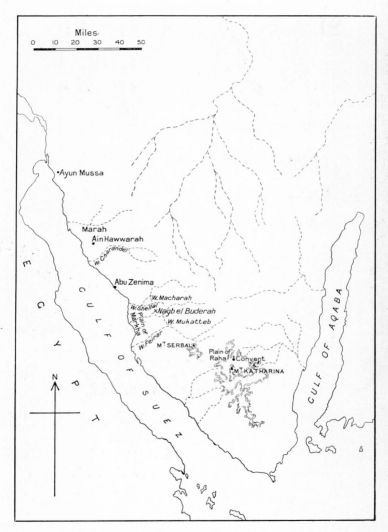

The Peninsular of Sinai.

SEARCH ON SINAI

The Story of Tischendorf's Life
and the Search for a lost Manuscript

By

Dr. LUDWIG SCHNELLER

Translated from the original *by*
DOROTHEE SCHRÖDER

Illustrated

THE EPWORTH PRESS
(Edgar C. Barton)
25-35 City Road, London, E.C.1

10 Trans

098822

ACKNOWLEDGEMENT

The Translator is indebted to the Manager of *The Times* for his kindness in giving permission to include the paragraph concerning the purchase of the *Codex Sinaiticus* on page 128.

CONTENTS

ILLUSTRATIONS

TRANSLATOR'S FOREWORD

THE story of the finding of the *Codex Sinaiticus* has been told many times before, but we do not apologize for sending out this little book with its immortal story, the story of a great and thrilling adventure of a man of God.

The author of *Search on Sinai* is Tischendorf's son-in-law, Dr. Schneller, who was encouraged to set down the story of Tischendorf's life by an old friend. She was the widow of a Pastor Bickel in Mönchsrot, a small village in Bavaria. For a long time past it had seemed to her that all the books written about Tischendorf and the *Codex Sinaiticus* were mainly for the scholars. She therefore begged Dr. Schneller to write the story ' for the German people as a whole, and not only for the scholars ', and she added, ' thousands would thank you for it '. Her words were prophetic. In its original German language this little book has been read over and over again by ' those who are interested to hear the long and varied history of our beloved New Testament, and by those to whom their Bible is their daily strength and portion.

The tale is told so simply that all can

understand the immense importance of Tischendorf's work.

We therefore send out this book in the hope that the strange story it tells may ' set the hearts aglow '. May it also be an encouragement to search still more diligently in those Holy Scriptures which by God's grace, through the medium of this man, were given to Christianity again.

YOUTH AND CHOICE OF A CAREER

THE Tischendorf family has lived in Saxony for centuries. According to an old tradition in the family one ancestor played a part in the history of the royal house of Saxony. In the year 1450 the two Saxon princes, Ernst and Albert, who later became the heads of separate branches of that family, were kidnapped. The Elector Friedrich of Saxony, known as ' The Gentle ', had seriously angered the otherwise gallant knight, Kunz von Kaufungen, who was his Lord Chamberlain. In vengeance the Lord Chamberlain decided to kidnap the two young princes. At dead of night he broke into the Castle of Altenburg, placed Prince Ernst in the hands of a confederate, while he himself, with Prince Albert, made his way through the forests in an attempt to cross the Bohemian border. Barely a mile from the border, however, he stopped to pick some berries for the hungry child. While thus occupied, a charcoal burner found them, and to him Prince Albert made himself known. When the stout charcoal burner heard who the child was, he started belabouring the kidnapper with his stirring-pole. His wife called together all the charcoal burners of the nearby charcoal pile, and they succeeded, with their united efforts, in overpowering the knight. Finally the princes were returned to their sorrowing father—who shortly after died—and the knight was beheaded.

The charcoal burner who thus succeeded in saving the young princes was a forebear of the Tischendorf family. When, therefore, many years later Konstantin Tischendorf was raised to the nobility, he chose as his coat-of-arms the one illustrated opposite the Foreword. It includes the charcoal burner with his stirring-pole, and, to illustrate Tischendorf's services in connection with the Holy Scriptures, it also includes a Bible with the Alpha and the Omega, as well as the sword of the Word of God and palm of peace.

There, in the State of Saxony, to which the family had remained true, Konstantin Tischendorf was born on January 18, 1815, in the little town of Lengenfeld. In the Gymnasium[1] of Plauen he laid the foundation for an unusually thorough knowledge of classical languages, upon which the whole of his future life's work was built. At the University of Leipzig, where he went in 1834, he eagerly continued his studies. Following his heart's desire he chiefly studied

[1] Grammar School.

theology, and prepared himself especially for the expounding of the New Testament. At the age of twenty-five, in the year 1840, he acquired permission to hold lectures at the University.

It was at this time that most of the famous German theologians, thinking they were rendering a service to historical truth, were doing their utmost to prove that the New Testament was not authentic. To achieve their ends they were using every means known to analytical science, in an attempt, so to speak, to extinguish the New Testament's lamp of life. Only four epistles of the Apostle Paul were considered genuine ; everything else was declared to be the work of later centuries. These learned gentlemen in particular condemned the four gospels, and least of all did the Gospel of St. John find favour in their eyes. It is true that there were still powerful witnesses at the German universities who energetically opposed these revolutionary assertions.

The resolute and faithful believers up and down the country, however, did not allow themselves to be misled by these alleged results of scientific investigation. A general uncertainty, nevertheless, began to make itself felt in many places, for the gospels, which were now publicly declared to be unreliable myths of a later date, were after all the only source from which to gain knowledge of

the life of Jesus. If, therefore, they were not
genuine, where could a sure foundation for faith
be found? What became of the sovereignty of the
Son of God, upon which after all the whole of
Christianity was based? It seemed as if the most
important foundations of the Christian faith had
begun to rock.

Several famous advocates of this school of
thought actually did draw the most drastic con-
clusions of the unreliability of the Gospels.

David Friderich Strauss wrote his *Life of
Jesus* (Leben Jesu) in which he declared the whole
story of Jesus to be a collection of fantastic legends.
This book, which received the widest publicity,
was welcomed by the enemies of the Christian
faith with great satisfaction.   To them it seemed
as if Christianity had at last been laid in its grave.
They were joined by the celebrated Frenchman
Renau, who, with a disregard of all scientific
investigation, degraded the story of Jesus to the
level of a fantastic novel.   Both in France and in
Germany his Life of Jesus was received with loud
acclamation.   Thus French frivolity and German
science joined together in an attempt to destroy
the Christian faith, as testified by the Gospels.

To-day scientific research stands on a different
footing. The result of that whole campaign
against the New Testament was only to establish

more irrefutably than ever the genuineness of the New Testament Scriptures. For over sixty years the most important critics have attacked the New Testament with the sharpest scientific weapons, never before used against any book. And the result? To-day the most daring and learned critics have to acknowledge that the whole of the New Testament, with the exception of a few unimportant details, is undeniably genuine and apostolic.

Even Professor Dr. von Harnack, the acknowledged leader of the critical school of thought, writes as follows concerning these scholarly errors in connection with the Epistles of St. Paul: ' When I began my theological studies about fifty-seven years ago, only those theologians were considered discerning men who admitted four only of the epistles to be genuine. Since then things have changed. Besides the First and Second Epistles to the Corinthians, Galatians and Romans, the authenticity of the First Thessalonians, Colossians, Philippians and Philemon is almost universally acknowledged. Of the epistles to the Churches, the Second of Thessalonians and Ephesians are still questionable. I recognize that there are certain difficulties here, particularly as regards Ephesians ; in my opinion, however, they are not insurmountable; and the points that speak for the authenticity decide the issue. Besides this it must be remembered that this collection is so old that the assumption that one of the epistles was a fake must give rise to serious doubt. Can one imagine that about the year 90, the Church of the Thessalonians received a letter, in a collection of epistles from Corinth, written by St. Paul, of which up till then they had had no knowledge, or that, about this date or earlier, they themselves had circulated a letter? At that time there were still people in the church who had known the Apostle and his relation to that community. It should therefore be considered highly probable that the original collection of ten epistles comprises only authentic writings.'

This is how things stand to-day. But in those days the conflict was terribly serious, and many people in the Christian communities allowed themselves to be confused by the alleged findings of science, as if the belief in the New Testament, and with it the belief in Jesus, had had its day.

This was the state of affairs as young Tischendorf found them when he started out on his theological career. He was convinced that at that moment nothing in theology was as important as the careful study of the oldest manuscripts of the New Testament, to prove their genuineness also from this angle, and thus to confute the opponents with the weapons of science. He looked upon it as the aim of his life to search for all the ancient manuscripts which might be proofs for the early existence and authenticity of the gospels. To reach this goal he was prepared to take endless trouble and make any sacrifice, even if his searchings led him into foreign countries. Thus, in his younger days, he had already chosen his real life's work. Blessed is he who in the decisive years recognizes his real vocation. Tischendorf was one of those lucky ones. In 1842, still little more than a youth, barely twenty-seven years of age, soon after the termination of his studies, he published his first critical edition of the Greek New Testament. This was welcomed by the learned men of science with undivided appreciation and pleasure as being a great advance on all previous writings.

Tischendorf wrote to his fiancée about it:

' At last I am on the eve of the completion of the New Testament. The fate of this piece of work I place in God's hands. Though I have behind me my habilitation and test lecture of the University of Leipzig, I would never like to be forced to make this habilitation (admission of an academical teacher into the faculty) the only foundation for the future development of my life. I am confronted with

B

a sacred task, the struggle to regain the original form of the New Testament.'

Thus early had Tischendorf realized his task, and he remained true to it all his life. Without deviating he followed the line he had chosen until the day of his death. And if one realizes how much he accomplished in forty-three years of untiring work, one feels compelled to admit that God had called him to the task.

2

FIRST SUCCESSES

To be able to understand the life work of Tischendorf, the reader must know something of the earliest history of the New Testament. In the beginning the Christian churches had as yet no New Testament. At their meetings and services the readings of Holy Scripture were taken from the Old Testament, the Prophets and the Psalms. For the rest, the teaching and witness of Jesus— the mainspring of the Christian Faith—was only passed on by word of mouth. These early churches still had the living witnesses of the deeds and words of Jesus with them—the apostles and their helpers. Besides this there was a verbal handing down of all that the apostles told of Jesus, which was recited to the congregations. Out of this verbal evidence, based on the personal experiences of the apostles, the three gospels seem to have emerged, so closely resembling each other that sometimes even the words are the same. The Gospel of St. Matthew was based on his collection of the Lord's sayings, the other two written by men who were not apostles, Mark and

Luke, who, however, wrote under the instruction or supervision of the apostles. The fourth Gospel, which has a trend of its own, was seemingly written by the aged Apostle John during the 'nineties of the first century. Later the letters of the apostles were added, which without doubt constitute the oldest parts of the New Testament. At first these letters were kept and treasured by the churches to which they were written, and read over and over again. Several decades later, particularly after the death of the apostles, other churches procured copies of these letters to read to the congregational meetings.

We have no information as to who first gathered all these writings together, and so formed the New Testament. On the other hand several of the earliest writers of the Christian era quote evidence, from which it is quite clear that such collections existed and met with much appreciation in the congregations, though they varied slightly in the sequence of their construction in the different churches. Thus the Bishop Clemence of Rome, in the year 95, takes it for granted that his readers are familiar with the epistles to the Corinthians, the Romans and the Hebrews. Bishop Ignatius of Antioch, who died about the year 115, in one of his letters which is still preserved, quotes passages from the epistles to the Corinthians and the Galatians, as well as from the Gospel of St. Matthew, and refers his readers to the epistles of St. Paul. Polycarp of Smyrna, who died in the year 155, refers to the epistles of St. Paul and quotes passages from the gospels of St. Matthew and St. Luke. Also the widely travelled Justin the Martyr, who died about the year 165, in his writings mentions not only the gospels, but also the Revelation of St. John. From all this, as well as from other evidences which I will pass over, it is clearly seen that the writings of the apostles were already in the hands of the churches at the end of the first century.

I must, however, mention the famous fragment of Muratori, an historian and librarian of Milan, who died in 1750. Muratori published the fragment of a manuscript from the latter half of the second century. This manuscript is the first known attempt at an authoritative collection of writings generally acknowledged as belonging to the New Testament. According to this manuscript the New Testament consisted of four gospels, thirteen epistles of St. Paul, the epistle of Jude and the Revelation of St. John. At the same time there is mention of the fact that a letter by Hermas, entitled ' The Shepherd ' was not permitted in the church service, in other words, was not recognized as apostolic. Besides this, several writings are mentioned which, though not considered apostolic, were yet occasionally made use of, such as two epistles of St. Paul to the churches in Laodicea and Alexandria, and also a revelation of St. Peter, which latter, however, was not recognized by all the churches. The epistle of St. James, which, as is well known, was not written by the apostle of that name, but by a brother of our Lord, and that to the Hebrews are missing as not being apostolic, while the epistle of Jude and the second and third epistles of John are treated as a supplement.

Irenaeus, whose death occurred in A.D. 202, mentions ' The Shepherd ' of Hermas as a part of the New Testament, whereas Tertullian, who died about twenty years later, tells us about an epistle of Barnabas, written about A.D. 100, of which he says, however, that it was not universally acknowledged. The reader must bear these writings of Hermas and Barnabas in mind as they come into the story again later.

Even in the fourth century the collection of the Scriptures of the New Testament was not complete. Eusebius, the famous ' Father of Church History ', a very learned and reliable man, who died A.D. 340, says that in his time the epistles of James and Jude, the second epistle of Peter and the second and third epistles of John were only considered authentic by some of the churches, whilst they were rejected by others. Other writings, such as the Acts of St. Paul,[1] 'The Shepherd' of Hermas, the Revelation of St. Peter, and also the Revelation of St. John, were doubtless considered unauthentic.

It was the great churchman Athanasius who, in the year 367, first declared the twenty-seven books, which to-day constitute the New Testament, to be the universally acknowledged Holy Scripture of the Christian Church. As several distinguished synods, through the passing of legal resolutions, pronounced themselves in favour of this finding, it has thus remained, even though equally distinguished scholars still choose to throw doubt on the authenticity of the above-mentioned Scriptures.

This collection of Holy Scriptures was now duplicated in ever growing numbers. Just as we now have printing works for these purposes, so in those days there were in existence big and famous writing establishments, where admirable writing experts made copies of all sorts of writings for the whole world. Our libraries still contain three thousand manuscripts of the New Testament,

---

[1] These are the writings of a certain Abdias about the history of St. Paul. They are, however, not genuine. While they are presented as if they were contemporary, they were actually not written until much later.

which all date from the eleven centuries before the invention of the printing-press. Later the Greek manuscripts were often printed, just as they came into the publisher's hand, without much editing. Only after the work done by the very able Württemberg theologian, Dr. Albrecht Bengel, more care was taken. In this direction too Tischendorf's life's work was to be that of a pioneer. His predecessors had already followed the principle that the nearer a manuscript stood in point of time to the original, namely, the apostolic writings, the more valuable and authoritative it was. His immediate distinguished predecessor in this direction, the Berlin scholar, Lachmann, had tried to reconstruct the New Testament with the aid of the oldest manuscripts, as it was used in the churches in the fourth century. These manuscripts, however, were not sufficiently known. The most important and oldest manuscripts known were the following:

I. The Alexandrian Manuscript in the British Museum in London called the Codex A, which, except for a few gaps, comprised the Old and the New Testaments. Just before Tischendorf's time this Codex had been published with the aid of British diligence and British money at a cost of £30,000. The date of this Codex is not before A.D. 450.

II. The Vatican Manuscript, Codex B, had been discovered earlier. Very little was known of this Codex

A palimpsest.

however, as the Pope would allow no one access to it with a view to making its precious contents known to science, through publication. This Codex B has gaps both in the Old and the New Testaments. It dates from the fourth century.

III. The Paris Palimpsest (twice-written parchment) or Codex C. As the reader will probably not know the meaning of palimpsest, I will explain it. A palimpsest is a manuscript parchment on which in olden times something had been written, and then in later centuries, because the parchment was expensive and because no one knew the value of the old manuscript, it had been used a second time. For this reason the first and older handwriting had of course to be erased and made illegible. This was achieved by treating with sharp acids. With the aid of the illustration the reader will get an idea of what a palimpsest in Greek looks like.

Such a palimpsest, and moreover a New Testament manuscript lay in the National Library in Paris. It was discovered that the original semi-erased writing dated from the first part of the fifth century, about the same time as the Alexandrian manuscript. In the twelfth century, after partial removal of the early writing, essays by Ephraem the Syrian—who died in A.D. 378, when principal of the theological school in Edessa in Mesopotamia—were written over it. During the process, however, the original writing had been so badly treated that its deciphering was a very hard task for the scholars. They had succeeded, after innumerable attempts, in discovering that the New Testament, or parts of it, had originally been written on the

parchment.   All attempts at deciphering it in detail,
however, remained fruitless. Capperonier, the director
of the library, finally declared that in his opinion no one
would ever manage to decipher the old manuscript,
hidden under the writings of Ephraem the Syrian.

IV.   Finally there was yet another manuscript, the
manuscript of Clermont, which had formerly belonged
to Bezas, but is now in the National Library in Paris.
It is known as the Codex Claramontanus, or Codex D;
it had, however, never been properly published.   In
1840 Tischendorf's famous predecessor, Lachmann,
declared that the Paris scientists would render an
immortal service to the knowledge of the New Testament if they could manage to publish a printed copy of
the Codex regius Ephraemi and the Claramontanus.
The Codex Claramontanus contains the complete
epistles of the Apostle Paul, in Greek and Latin.   It got
its name from the fact that it came from a monastery in
Clermont in France.

The first piece of work which Tischendorf
courageously undertook was a critical editing of
the whole New Testament, after comparing all
old manuscripts then known.   His audacity in
undertaking such a tremendous piece of work, at
so young an age, brought him not only ridicule
but enmity from many of the Leipzig professors.
To his fiancée he wrote :

LEIPZIG, October 1840.

' At last I have reached the eve of the completion of my New Testament.   This gigantic

undertaking has weighed heavily on me, and later on it will seem unbelievable, even to me, that I could write a book in less than a year which will bring me both curses and blessings, disgrace and glory. I lay its future in God's hand. Though jealousy and narrow mindedness cast suspicion upon me, I know I have struggled, in an earnest and holy endeavour, though all my strength is but weakness. But I also have influential and respected friends. My beloved Bishop Dräseke has written to me so warmly. He welcomes my *Novum Testamentum Græce* as " the foundation stone of my literary immortality ". On the occasion of the Swearing of Allegiance he wants to present a copy of the book to the King of Prussia. And the Prussian Minister Eichhorn is in consequence going to grant me a personal interview. If others suspect me of following any other than a heaven-sent goal, you must not believe it.'

After the publication of this first book, the forerunner of many other and larger ones, he immediately started on another task. The *Codex D*, or *Claramontanus*, in Paris, and the Paris Palimpsest, *Codex C*, gave him no peace. It is true that the notable representatives of science had declared the deciphering of the latter an impos-

sibility.   But he wanted to see for himself.   Once
again distinguished voices raised themselves in
protest against him and his undertaking.   But he
wrote to his fiancée:

    ' I have lived through a year of tremendous
aspirations, anxieties and heartache, but also
of exaltation.   In the affair concerning my
journey I have had one disappointing experi-
ence after another.   You see, I cannot carry
through my plans for Paris without a stipend
from our Ministry of Public Worship and
Education.   Several are trying to prevent this,
but I am not going to despair.   I believe with
Christian joy that the Father in Heaven loves
me, for he chastises me.   What after all is the
crime for which I am suffering?   That I leave
the comfortable path of study, where also I
might achieve something excellent, and turn
my face to the unusual.   But before God I feel
it in the depths of my soul, it is not a conceited,
arrogant desire on my part, but it is an inspired,
highminded endeavour which I myself cannot
resist.

    ' In October, therefore, I go to Paris after
the Ministry has granted me the stipend, and
my beloved brother has promised me an equal
sum.

    ' By using all my talents, I intend to try and

support myself as much as possible. And then I have other aspirations and aims. One lies as far away as Rome! I am prepared for anything and throw myself, a daring though cautious swimmer, into the whirlpool.'

Thus he turned his face confidently towards Paris, to attempt a task which as yet no one had been able to accomplish. And this was his first step in a career which, from then on, carried him forward from success to success.

3

GROWING SUCCESSES

IN the autumn of 1840, in his twenty-seventh
year, Tischendorf travelled to Paris. There, in
the public library lay the two precious manuscripts, whose acquaintance we have already
made, the *Codex Ephraemi* and the *Codex Claramontanus*, with their secrets not yet unravelled.
It was these manuscripts which drew him to the
great city by the Seine. The publication of the
Claramontanus would not present any great
difficulties. All the greater, however, would
they be in the case of the *Codex Ephraemi*, and
seemed, in fact, insurmountable. When the
young scholar asked for the manuscript at the
library, it was certainly very readily produced.
The librarians, however, with patronizing smiles,
said to him: ' The most learned and famous
scholars have worked on this palimpsest without
success. Only about six years ago we very carefully treated the parchment with chemicals, hoping to make the old partly erased and covered
handwriting legible again, but without success.
If you, as a young beginner, think you can do

better, by all means try your luck. But we can tell you in advance; you will achieve nothing.'

And yet, here at last had come the knight who was destined to wake this sleeping beauty from a thousand years' sleep. He was well equipped for his bold undertaking, not only through his zeal and scientific knowledge, but also through his eyesight. When his mother had been in good hopes, she had been much moved by the sight of an unhappy blind man. Since then it had always been the pious woman's prayer: 'Lord, do not let my child be blind.' And like an answer to this prayer, her son Konstantin was blessed with eyesight of such unusual sharpness as is rarely found.

He set about his work with determination. At first it also seemed to him as if the solving of the problem was an impossibility. But with un-daunted will-power and his sharp eyes he would not allow himself to be discouraged. It was a gigantic undertaking. Day after day he sat in the library with the ancient Codex before him and examined the pale, washed-out Greek letters, which showed very faintly under the sturdy Syrian characters. Letter after letter was scru-tinized, all possibilities considered, until at last the right one was found. And thus it progressed, letter by letter, line by line, page by page, through two long years.

With astonishment the librarians watched the successes of the young German scholar. They showed him greater and greater respect and helped him in every possible way. And his task actually did end in a complete triumph. Tischendorf had accomplished that which, according to the greatest experts, no living man could ever successfully carry out. When, early in 1843, he left the capital, he had the satisfaction of carrying with him a printed copy of the Old and New Testament, according to the hitherto mysterious palimpsest of the fifth century. And with the other treasure too, the *Codex Claramontanus*, which contained the epistles of the Apostle Paul, he was successful, and published it some years later, making it accessible to the world of science.

Amongst the scientists these successes created a great stir. Everyone was praising the new light which had arisen in the world of palaeography (the science of ancient writings), and all over Europe the name of Tischendorf was mentioned with profound admiration.

The libraries in which he wanted to investigate old Bible manuscripts now most willingly opened their doors to him. Further and further he extended his searchings. He travelled to London and to Holland, made not only valuable discoveries, but enlarged his knowledge and

Konstantin von Tischendorf
at the time of his Paris sojourn.

increased his capacity for judging ancient manuscripts. He then went to Switzerland and Italy, and explored the libraries in Venice, Milan, Turin, Modena, Florence, and Naples. Of course he also went to Rome, where lay in the papal palace, still withheld from the investigations of science, the most precious of the then known manuscripts of the New Testament, the *Codex Vaticanus*. So as to assist him, the Saxon Prince Johann, the King of Saxony, as well as the Archbishop of Paris, and the French Minister in Dresden, had given him the warmest letters of recommendation to the Pope. Gregory XVI, who had already heard of the young scholar's successes, received him kindly, and seemed inclined to let him have the famous Codex, with a view to publishing its contents. But in Rome even the Pope cannot always do as he likes. The guardian of the treasure, Cardinal Mai, who also intended publishing the Codex, did not wish that honour to go to anyone else and succeeded in frustrating the Pope's intention. Tischendorf was only allowed to have the venerable old manuscript for six hours, and that of course was of no use. But where he failed then, he succeeded later. In 1867 he published this manuscript also, under the title of *Novum Testamentum Vaticanum*.

C

During the next few years, important publications succeeded one another at short intervals. In 1846 he published, under the name of *Monumenta Sacra Inedita* the result of all his investigations and discoveries, which were so valuable both to the Christian Church and to Bible researches. In particular, he brought out ever new and better editions of his Greek New Testament, which all the great scholars welcomed with greatest appreciation, and which, from then onwards, became the foundation for the study of the Holy Book in the original language throughout the world.

4

THE FIRST JOURNEY TO SINAI IN 1844

THE passion of his life had seized the young Leipzig scholar and would not let him go. He wanted to do everything in his power to restore to Christianity the original wording of the New Testament. He had searched all the libraries of the Western World which seemed likely to serve his purpose. Now he turned his interest to the East.

That was quite natural. After all, from where did all these ancient manuscripts come, such as the Paris *Codex Ephraemi*, the *Vaticanus*, the *Claramontanus* and all the other old Greek writings which were guarded in the European libraries as great treasures? All from the East, where knowledge and science, and especially Christianity, were first fostered. Again and again, when Tischendorf sat before one of those ancient manuscripts, his thoughts went to those far distant lands, where they had once been written by a hand long since turned to dust. Was it not

possible that in some episcopal see, in libraries, in
monasteries or in hidden corners of these monasteries yet more treasures lay, always in danger of
destruction at the hands of ignorant monks?
Could they not still be saved? Was it not a duty
to make the attempt, while there was still time?
These thoughts grew on him, until he could no
longer resist them. He decided to journey out to
the East, a merchant, seeking a precious pearl.

In December 1843 he wrote to his fiancée about
his plans:

'The Ministry of Public Worship and
Education has equipped me wonderfully for
my trip to the East. I received this news with
tears of joy. I felt as if I were going towards a
great and marvellous feast. How God has
blessed me! Jerusalem will cast a transfiguring
glow around future days. The golden
fruit of this journey hangs over an abyss. But
that is just what makes me so happy: that I
may fight in this battle, to attempt to win a
blessing for the church, for science and the
Fatherland, together with immortal laurels.
Should I succumb, I should do so in the most
glorious endeavour, and I should quickly find,
instead of the empty grave, the Hero of the
Easter Morn. From here in Verona I intend
going to Milan, in January to Turin, and in

Angelika Zehme, Tischendorf's fiancée.

March to Leghorn, from where I take ship to Alexandria. From there I go to Sinai, Jerusalem, Constantinople, to the holy mount of Athos, and back to Leipzig via Greece and Trieste.'

A journey of this sort was not so easy nor so comparatively cheap in those days as it is to-day. It was a tremendous undertaking, which aroused widespread comment. For the twenty-nine year old university professor, who knew nothing of the East, it was a great step to take. But even the greatest difficulties did not prevent him from following the promptings of the still, small voice.

In the April of 1844 he left Leghorn in Italy for Egypt on his first visit. Here also there were old monasteries to be visited, dating from times when monastic life was at its height. They had, however, been plundered by the attacks of the wild hordes of Mohammed. It was therefore Mount Sinai above everything else which attracted him like a powerful magnet. What was it that drew him there so irresistibly? It was the monastery, more than thirteen hundred years old, that lies at the foot of Mount Sinai. Above all other monasteries of the East it had the great advantage of being the only one that had never been destroyed, not even during the triumphal march of the Mohammedan conquerors. On the roof of the

monastery there is a small Mosque, a Mohammedan place of prayer.   The clever monks, it is
said, built the mosque when the warriors of the
false prophet were approaching, and this saved
the monastery from plunder and destruction, for,
according to Mohammed, no mosque must ever
be destroyed.   And so it was that the monastery,
which had been founded by Emperor Justinian
in the year 530 at the foot of the Holy Mount, had
remained unmolested for over a thousand years.
Besides this it was so shut off from the world by
the lonely desert which surrounded it that wild
hordes hardly ever found their way there.   On
these important facts Tischendorf founded his
hope that he might there find some precious old
manuscripts of the New Testament.

Like everyone who first sets foot in the country
of the Pyramids, Tischendorf on landing in
Alexandria, surveyed this strange world with
astonishment.   But the Nile did not hold him for
long.   Mount Sinai, the old mountain of God,
with its precipitous rocks, was constantly in his
mind.   By the middle of May, therefore, he was
already on his way, travelling through the desert.

It was a journey such as the Leipzig professor
had never before dreamed of making.   There
was no railway, no road, no vehicle.   On the
back of a camel he rode from Cairo to the

Monastery of St. Catharine, at the foot of Mount Sinai, in twelve days. He was accompanied by a dragoman, who acted as interpreter, and besides this the small caravan counted three Bedouins and four camels. Early, before dawn, they started, then from ten o'clock until five they rested in tents because of the heat, and from five until eleven o'clock they rode on again. About midnight the weary traveller laid down to sleep, naturally tired out by the unaccustomed camel ride. At night the tent was not put up, for it was warm enough in the desert, and one did not need the canvas to ward off the heat of the sun as in the daytime. His bed was then surrounded by his baggage, a loaded gun lay next to him, and one Bedouin had to stand guard. Above him the starry heavens of the East shone in incredible glory, and the camels grunted in the distance.

From the very first day the tremendous heat oppressed the traveller, for May is the hottest month of the year in those parts. He felt as if he were in a turkish bath. Added to this a sudden breeze, which blew across from the Red Sea, carried off his straw hat, this indispensable guard against the hot rays of the sun. The three Bedouins chased after it, but returned after three-quarters of an hour without having retrieved it. Without a hat, however, the journey could not be continued, so back they went once more and searched all night, until by eight o'clock next morning they came back with it.

The caravan was of course supplied with everything that was necessary for a twelve-day journey through the desert, during which one could buy nothing. There were cooking and eating utensils, salt, groceries, matches, the most ordinary things, which one does not usually have to think about on a journey. Above all, there was the water, which was carried in earthenware jugs by one of the camels. The Suez Canal had not yet been made, so the camels and their riders waded through the Red Sea at about the same spot where the Israelites had crossed dry shod. Their first camp in Asia was at the Wells of Moses, Ayun Mussa, under palms and by the fresh springs. It is said that Moses and the Israelites, after gaining their freedom, also had their first camp here.

From here their path led them through desolate, waterless tracts of land, where once the wandering Israelites had languished and all but despaired. In Ain Hawarah they came to the old Marah with its bitter water, and in Wadi Gharandel they saw the lovely Elim of the Israelite wanderings, with its palms and its wells. On the following day the grand mountain range

The pass of Nugb el Budra.

of Sinai came into view for the first time. Through a narrow gap in the mountains, whose rocky walls rose sheer towards the sky, they once more reached the Red Sea. Like Moses and his wandering people three thousand years before, so Tischendorf once more spent the night by the seashore, under the immense rocky walls of Ras Abu Zenima. In the time of the Pharaohs there was a busy harbour at this place. To-day it is dead and deserted.

From here, on lonely paths, between majestic, chalk-white mountains, the travellers traversed the plain of Markha, and then penetrated deeper into the hills and valleys of the Sinai mountains.

It is not necessary here to describe more fully the grand beauty of the scenery. I have already done so in my book *Through the Desert to Sinai*. I will therefore only just mention the most interesting parts of the road.

After crossing the plain of Markha the road led over the wild mountain pass of Nugb el Budra and the Wadi Shellal into the ancient hills. Here the oldest known formations of the earth's crust looked down on them, gneiss, granite, mica, syenite, and porphyry. Before I myself rode through here, I had never thought it was possible that bare rocky walls, devoid of vegetation, could have such unearthly colours. The mountain giants glowed in the richest hues: red, green, yellow, white, black and chocolate-brown. In the distance the proudest peak of the Sinai mountains, Serbal, rose up impressively. Steeper and ever steeper the mountain peaks joined themselves into long ranges. Thus Tischendorf rode over the wild part of Nugb el Budra with its steplike gradients, through the rocky channel of Wadi Mararah, closed in by walls of porphyry, where the Pharaohs had their turquoise mines, through the famous Valley of the Suscriptions, Wadi Mukaettaeb, with its strange characters on the rocks, on through the wonderful oasis of the Wadi Feiran,[1] over which the Amalekites and the Israelites under Joshua had fought, and where one still finds manna under the trees. For scenery it is one of the most beautiful places one could find in the five continents. And Tischendorf rode on with wonder in his eyes, through this magnificent world, until, on the twelfth day, in the distance he saw the goal of his dreams, the Monastery of St. Catharine.

On emerging from the narrow mountain path, he saw before him a valley, above which, rising up into the cloudless blue of the heavens, the majestic mountains towered, which by Jews, Christians, and Mohammedans alike is revered

[1] See illustration facing page 64.

as the place of the law-giving of Sinai.   Soon he
stood in the wide plain of Raha, above which the
northern, bare rock of Mount Sinai rises precipi-
tously.   To the right of it on the edge of the sandy
desert he could see a few green patches, a most
surprising sight in the dry desert.   They were the
two gardens of the monastery.   Behind them in
a narrow gorge the monastery itself appeared,
looking like a fortress.   Tischendorf's heart beat
high, as he saw before him the place about which,
latterly, he had dreamed day and night.   The
camels were urged to a fast trot, and by ten o'clock
the caravan stood under the stone walls of the
Sinai monastery.[1]   After repeatedly calling, a
door, which looked like a window, was opened
above their heads, about twelve yards from the
ground.   A basket was let down on the end of a
rope, and was pulled up again after Tischendorf
had put into it a letter of recommendation from
the monastery in Cairo.   The letter was examined and found in order.   Then, as there was in
those days no entrance on ground level, the
strong rope was let down again, this time
attached to a crossbar.   The guests had to climb
astride this and were thus hoisted through the air.
This was a strictly enforced custom to safeguard
the monastery from raids.

[1] See illustration facing page 96.

5

THE FIRST SOJOURN AT THE MONASTERY OF ST. CATHARINE

THE Monastery of Sinai was in the first place founded in memory of the Law-giving on Mount Sinai. Its name, however, it received from St. Catharine. One of the majestic mountains of the Sinai range, the Gebel Katherina, is also named after her.

Who was this St. Catharine? She was not St. Catharine of Siena, the patron saint of the Dominican Order, nor St. Catharine of Bologna, patron saint of the Franciscans, but Catharine of Alexandria, the ' ever pure ' as her Greek name denotes, the revered saint of the East. According to the legend, she was of princely parentage and lived in Alexandria. She was supposed to have been very beautiful, learned, unusually conversant with the sciences, of humble faith, and deeply devoted to her Saviour. The Roman Emperor Maximin (307-313), one of the last persecutors of Christianity, and at one time joint emperor with Constantine the Great, met her in Alexandria, took a tremendous fancy to the beautiful young girl, and persecuted her with unseemly proposals.

To save herself from the Emperor's aggressiveness and power, St. Catharine fled into the lonely Valleys of Sinai, where, far from corruption and vice, she intended consecrating her life to God. But here, too, the Emperor's spies found her. She was taken back to Alexandria by force and there imprisoned, until she might see reason and renounce her stubborn Christian faith. Fifty heathen philosophers were sent to see her in prison, to undermine her faith. All of them, however, were gloriously vanquished by her, who was a master of argument, and two hundred Praetorians were won for the Crucified, all by the force of the prisoner's conviction. At last the Emperor lost patience, and ordered St. Catharine's execution. Quietly resigned, with prayers and praise, St. Catharine followed the executioners to the scaffold. There the beautiful martyr's limbs were fixed to the wheel. But the wheel broke, as if it refused to be used for such a despicable execution. So the hangman had to take the sword and behead her. And thus she died in the year 307, a victim of the last and worst persecution which passed over Christianity before Constantine lifted the banner of the Cross over the whole of the Roman Empire.

Angels, so the legend goes on to tell, came down, with gentle hands lifted the body of the saint, and carried it away over land and sea to the place where once she had found refuge, and laid it down on the highest peak of the peninsula, which from that day in her honour was given the name of Gebel Katherina. They say that partridges followed the saint, thus carried by the angels, over ocean and mountains, a modest and touching funeral train, so that at least some creature from the animal world might honour her thus, while men were unable to do so.   Tired out with their flight over sea, valleys and mountains, the birds came down on the waterless height, and gathered round the body of the saint. As a reward for the kindly service they had rendered, God made a spring rise on the parched heights. To this day that spring bears the name Bir Eshunar (spring of the partridges).   Since then the memory of St. Catharine sanctifies this highest peak of the Sinai range, an illustration of which will be found facing page 88. With its black and dark green rocks, the mountain solemnly points to heaven, a mighty monument to the faithful witness of Alexandria.

Legends and poetry have woven stories around St. Catharine.   Painters have often portrayed her, giving her as symbols, besides a crown, a broken wheel in one hand, and in the other a book to symbolize her wisdom. As Queen of Philosophers the philosophical faculty of the university of Paris has even adopted her as patron saint. The monks of the Sinai monastery believe to possess the most precious thing of all, however, St. Catharine's body, which they once found upon the Gebel Katherina. They laid it in a valuable coffin and buried it in the chapel of the monastery. Since then the monastery bears the world famous name of St. Catharine.

But quite apart from this legend the Monastery of St. Catharine is a very remarkable, if not the most remarkable, monastery in the world. In the year 530 the Emperor Justinian had the monastery built like a fortress as a protection for the hermits and desert saints who lived round about. Later on, when the hermits could hold out no longer against the thieving Bedouins, they all entered the monastery. That is why even to-day, as our illustration shows, it looks just a fortress. A high wall of granite, in the shape of an irregular quadrangle, surrounds the buildings. We have already heard that the monks further protected themselves against robbers by having the entrance door several stories up, so that one could only gain admittance by being hoisted through the air by means of a windlass.

On reaching the interior of the monastery one finds a collection of different kinds of buildings, erected without any particular plan, which makes it difficult to find one's way about. In the fourteenth century, whenever necessity arose, another building was added indiscriminately to the existing ones. The church, halls, living houses, cells, galleries, balconies, open yards and terraces: subways, which ran under the houses like the tunnels of a mole: and over it all the two towers, one the well-built Christian bell-tower, and the other the somewhat decrepit little Mohammedan minaret. From these two towers the Cross and the Crescent together look down on to the strange Church State of the Fathers of Mount Sinai. Some of the cells are built like swallows' nests, high up in the battlements of the fortress wall, so that the monks can go for dangerous walks along the highest ramparts.

The Monastery of St. Catharine is not the only one belonging to this Order. The Fathers of Mount Sinai have monasteries in Suez, Tor by the Red Sea, Cairo, where their archbishop lives, in Syria, Crete, in the Caucasus and in the Balkans. In the latter, however, they have lost a great deal of their large fortunes through the World War. The parent monastery, however, is the Monastery of St. Catharine. The Holy

The Monastery of St. Catherine.

Fathers have dwelt here for over a thousand years. If like St. Catharine, these monks had filled their lives with serious intellectual occupation, even such monastic life could have been fruitful and full of blessing. There are here, however, no lecture halls, where a host of eager young disciples might sit at the feet of their masters in the quest of truth : there are no monks versed in penmanship as in olden days, who by their beautiful writings enriched the world's wealth. No great thinkers peopled the corridors and galleries of the spacious monastery buildings; no cells are here where mental struggles are fought, such as Luther's in Erfurt. The whole life of the monastery is empty as a burnt-out crater. Religious life has deteriorated into a daily burden of prescribed and ungraciously observed devotions, and to a meagre bill of fare according to detailed rules for fast days.

Following the rule laid down by St. Basilius, all wine is forbidden; the crafty monks, however, so the Abbot or Archimandrite himself once told me, had discovered that no rule forbade distilled liquor, and that it was therefore allowed. And the Holy Fathers were certainly experts in distilling a sort of Araki, or palm brandy, which they repeatedly offered to me. It is unfortunately the only product of the ' spirit ' which they can take

D

the credit for. Divine Service, consisting of an endless number of liturgies, is celebrated eight times each day, and everyone must be present four times daily, twice in the daytime and twice at night. Even Tischendorf, who, because of his work, tried to get on the right side of the Fathers, wrote in his first letter to his fiancée, with a sigh:

> ' I have now been in the St. Catharine Monastery eight days. But oh, these monks! If I had military strength and power, I should be doing a good deed if I threw this rabble over the walls. It is sad to see how man carries his baseness and wretchedness into the lofty grandeur of this mountain world! '

These were certainly bad conditions, especially for his particular task, making the prospects rather hopeless, for if the monastery really possessed any old manuscripts, who of all these people could have appreciated their value?

We must, however, have a look around the monastery. Its foremost sanctuary is the low lying ' Church of the Transfiguration'. This is one of the most remarkable churches in the world, in the first place because of its age. Fourteen hundred years ago it was built by the Emperor Justinian, in the middle of the lonely desert, and yet with all the splendour of the then highly developed Byzantine architecture. Behind the altar is the chapel in which the greatest treasure of the monastery lies, the head and hand of St. Catharine. A few steps farther down there is another chapel, of unparalleled sanctity, that of 'The Burning Bush', in which God once appeared to Moses. Everyone, therefore, who wishes to enter, must first remove his shoes, remembering the words: ' Put off thy shoes from off thy feet, for the place whereon thou standest is holy ground.'

The surroundings of the monastery are magnificent. Looking up from the monastery courtyard, one sees the great red mountains of granite rise up into the blue heavens, at sunrise and sunset bathed in burning gold.

The reader can well imagine that during this visit to the monastery, which lasted several weeks, Tischendorf also climbed these lofty heights of Sinai. Up there on the summit there is an indescribably grand view. One can see, or easily construct in one's mind, the Peninsula of Sinai, lying between the two arms of the Red Sea. In the west shimmers the green surface of the Red Sea, and beyond it are the African hills. To the east, beyond the Gulf of Aqaba, are the mountains of Arabia. Wonderful is the view of the silent, lonely mountain world, surrounded by the peaks of bare hills and ranges.   They are like a wild, fearful, rocky ocean, once thrown heavenward in black and red-brown liquid waves, when our earth was under the pressure of primeval fiery forces, before being petrified into solid rock.   He who believes this spot to be the spot from which, as from God's pulpit, Moses received the Law, will be overcome by a deep feeling of reverence and awe.

After such a visit to the summit of the Mountain of Moses, Tischendorf wrote to his fiancée:

' How beautiful is Sinai, and everything about it! I have never seen anything grander than the precipitous towering, rocky walls of granite that make up the mountain range of Sinai. With this letter, my dear, I enclose a slip of paper which I wrote for you while I was up there on the lofty summit.'

This slip of paper, which is still preserved, contains the following words:

' I am praying on the stone whereon Moses prayed. The spirit of God surrounded him. Oh, that that spirit would permeate me with its eternal power! To-day is Whit Sunday. How happy I am! The hot light of the sun is breaking through the mist which envelops the mountains. I am hoping that this may be a

symbol of yours and my future, my Angelika!
That is what I will pray for from the Father of
all Prayer, pray for you and me. I greet you
thus, my beloved heart, from the height of
Sinai.'

Much as Tischendorf at times enjoyed giving
himself up to these mighty impressions, they were
nevertheless, for him, of secondary importance.
His greatest sanctuary was the library of the
monastery in which he hoped to find a treasure of
incalculable value, the oldest handwriting of the
New Testament. This sanctuary was, however,
not so well furnished as the other celebrated
churches and chapels of the monastery. On the
contrary, it was a poor place, to which no one in
the monastery paid much attention. (I thought
that even the present room, which is better
furnished than in Tischendorf's time, still seemed
rather pathetic.)

With high expectations, Tischendorf entered
this library, the goal and aim of many years'
longing. Around its four walls on wooden
stands were many books and manuscripts. Here
the treasure must lie. He took down the books
one by one and examined them carefully. But
even though he found some things of value, a
handwritten New Testament was not amongst

them. Deeply disappointed, he finally gave up
the search. He had seen everything there was to
see, and yet had not found what he was looking
for with such burning desire.

As he was about to leave the library, deeply
discouraged, he saw in the middle of the room an
enormous wastepaper basket which contained all
kinds of rubbish, papers and scraps of books. So
as not to miss anything, he emptied out the basket
and investigated its contents. Smilingly, the
librarian Kyrillos stood by and said: ' Lately
that basket has twice been filled with such rubbish, but we have thrown it all into the fire so as
to get it out of our way. This lot will also be in
the fire soon.' And while he spoke Tischendorf
was picking out one valuable piece after the other,
and examining it.

Suddenly he got a pleasant shock. There in
the basket lay a number of parchment sheets of a
larger size, written with Greek characters. His
expert eye recognized them at once as being of
very early date. From his European searchings
he knew the characteristics of the oldest manuscripts. There was no doubt about it; here was
a really ancient manuscript. With some emotion
he studied the contents. And what did he find?
There were 129 large sheets of parchment out of
the *Septuaginta*, the well-known Greek translation

of the Old Testament. Though it was not the New Testament, which he had come all this way in the hope of finding, nevertheless, this discovery was of immense value.

As the contents of the basket were intended for the fire, he had little difficulty in persuading the monks to give him some of this rubbish, namely, the small portion of loose leaves which lay together, in all 43 pages. With this treasure he immediately went to his room and pored over it. The Abbot, as soon as he realized their value, refused to part with the remainder of the 129 pages. He permitted Tischendorf, however, to note down the contents of the 86 pages of the Old Testament, and, in the case of a few pages, to make a careful copy.

It would seem, that before the year 1844 no one in the monastery had taken particular notice of these sheets of parchment, or to have had any idea of their value. And yet without doubt they must have lain there since the founding of the monastery thirteen hundred years before. It was a dreadful thought to Tischendorf that in all probability quite a lot of equally precious sheets of parchment, perhaps even the New Testament, for which he was searching, had been thrown into the fire. Before his departure he therefore impressed upon the otherwise friendly and obliging librarian Kyrillos, that it was his sacred duty carefully to look after the remaining 86 pages, to collect any others he might find, and guard them well. He held out the prospect that he might later return to Sinai, after persuading the monastery's powerful fellow believer, the Tsar of Russia,[1] to show the monastery some special favour, for the sake of this treasure.

[1] The Tsar of Russia was a Greek Orthodox, as were also the members of the Order of the Fathers of Sinai.

6

THE SECOND JOURNEY TO SINAI IN
1853

IN 1845 Tischendorf returned to Leipzig. Besides the Monastery of Sinai, he had visited quite a number of monasteries in the East, and had brought back with him a number of valuable handwritings of all sorts, which set the sciences of theology and philosophy many new tasks.

He immediately developed an astonishing activity with a view to making these manuscripts accessible to science. Above all things he started on the precious 43 sheets of parchment of the Old Testament. They turned out to be the very oldest handwriting which the world possesses. After they had been carefully edited, including their many corrections and additions, accompanied by a facsimile, they were placed in the Leipzig University library, and received the name *Codex Friderico-Augustanus*, in honour of the King of Saxony. Besides this there were publications of all the handwritings found and bought in the East, Greek, Syrian, Koptic, Arabian and Georgian.

Scientists marvelled as one after another these treasures, that had lain in some corner of a monastery in the distant desert, came to light.

Tischendorf did not tell, however, where he had found those 43 sheets of parchment. If, in particular, the English had got to know the place, they would have gone there straightaway to buy the treasure with lavishly spent English money, and have taken it to the British Museum in London. Already in those days it was considered almost a creed in England that the best in the world should naturally belong to the British.

Tischendorf therefore kept his secret, and none knew in what isolated spot these sheets had been found. But it was just this that drew him to Sinai again. There and nowhere else, he told himself, will my life's work be crowned, if I succeed in lifting the whole treasure. At first he tried to reach his goal through the friendly and reliable Dr. Pruner-Bey, physician-in-ordinary to the Viceroy of Egypt. Tischendorf offered him a considerable sum of money with which to purchase the remaining 86 parchment pages. Dr. Pruner-Bey, however, informed him through a reliable messenger: ' Since your departure from the monastery they know well enough that they have a treasure. The more you offer, the less likely will they be to let you have it.'

After receiving this news Tischendorf decided on a second journey to Sinai. As the purchase seemed out of the question, he at least wanted to copy the remaining 86 pages of the Greek Old Testament, as well as a number of other hand-writings which he had seen there, with a view to publishing their contents. In this way at least the original text of these precious pages would be saved, in case the pages themselves were destroyed through the carelessness of the monks. He confidentially told his secret to the then Saxon Minister of Public Worship, and readily received the necessary funds for the trip—which in those days was expensive—from the State Treasury. About New Year 1853 Tischendorf left for Egypt. At the beginning of February, after an absence of nine years, he was once more back in the Sinai Monastery.

How disappointed was he to find that no one in the whole monastery knew anything about the 86 pages he had left behind! Not even the pleasant and obliging librarian Kyrillos could remember what had happened to the precious pages which Tischendorf, nine years before, had pulled out of the dangerous basket and given into his care. He had no doubt that Kyrillos was honest. But it was obvious the treasure had disappeared. He could only explain its disappearance by imagining that in the meantime some other European had got wind of the whole thing, had bought the treasure without the previous knowledge of the librarian Kyrillos, and had removed it to England or Russia. It was to be expected that in due course Europe would be surprised by the publication of the old manuscript.

One little trace of the manuscript, however, he did find. In a Greek codex with stories of the saints Tischendorf found a small piece of parchment, not as large as a hand, being used as a bookmark. The writing on this bit of parchment showed the same ancient characters as the 43 pages he already had and contained a few verses of the twenty-fourth chapter of Genesis. That was proof that originally a complete handwriting of the Old Testament must have existed. But how did this discovery help him? It seemed obvious that someone else had taken the manuscript and that for all time he would have to abandon the hope of acquiring it.

Incidentally this failure was partly compensated for by other lucky finds in different countries of the East. In Cairo, Alexandria, Jerusalem, Laodicea, Smyrna, Constantinople, on the Holy Mount of Athos in Macedonia, he found sixteen palimpsests, several Greek uncial handwritings (writing with capital letters), a number of Greek,

Koptic, heiratical and hieroglyphic papyrus manuscripts, also some old Syrian and Arabian parchment manuscripts and a collection of Karaitic documents.

With this rich harvest he returned home from his voyage of discovery in the summer of 1853. Once more publications followed each other, all of which were welcomed with enthusiasm by the world of science. In 1857 the seventh edition of Tischendorf's large Greek New Testament in two volumes was finished, and was extensively circulated throughout the world. The untiring Tischendorf got through a great deal of work during this time. He added a new collection of a thousand-year-old Greek documents of the New and Old Testaments to the ' Library of Original Christian Documents ' which he had begun in 1842 with the Paris palimpsest. He now also published the fact that besides the 43 parchment pages he had also found another 86 pages at Sinai and had saved them from being burnt, so as to have it on record that he had been the first discoverer. Though his great hopes of finding also the oldest New Testament had been in vain, he could, however, in other ways be very proud of the successes of his journeys.

At the time, on his journey home, he had written to his wife from Cairo:

' In spite of the failure of my greatest ambition, I have nevertheless been crowned with grace and mercy, far beyond all my expectations. I am bringing home more than ten ancient palimpsests, amongst which are two particularly precious ones, one of the Old and the other of the New Testament. The first, dating from the fifth century [also the second bears this date], is a companion to the *Codex Friderico-Augustanus*. I intend calling it the *Codex Johannes* after our Crown Prince. Amongst these palimpsests, some of my greatest treasures are three uncial manuscripts from the ninth century, two of the gospels and one of Genesis. Praise the Lord with me! I must believe that I am about His work, since He blesses me thus.'

In Leipzig he waited from day to day to hear that some lucky one, who had forestalled him in the quest for the 86 pages and carried them off to England or Russia, had published his great find. But strangely enough nothing was heard about it. Had he been mistaken in his suspicions? Was the treasure still lying somewhere in the Sinai monastery untouched, forgotten, neglected and threatened with destruction?

7

THE THIRD JOURNEY TO SINAI IN 1859

THE publication, on the part of some foreigner, of the 86 pages which he left behind at Sinai, and which he expected with such anxious suspense, did not take place. Could it be possible? Could the incalculably valuable pages after all still be lying in that distant monastery? And if that were the case, would Tischendorf not have to go back there again and search still more thoroughly? Could he leave that treasure in the hands of the ignorant monks, after having once saved it from the fire? The thought left him no peace, and at last he decided to undertake the journey for the third time in search of the old document.

This time, however, he wanted to be in every way well prepared, better than on the previous occasions. He knew that nothing would please the Fathers of Mount Sinai more, or make them more amiable, than if he came to them in the name of their powerful fellow-believer, the Tsar of Russia. For him, whom they placed high above all the powerful ones of the earth, they would do anything. With the consent of the

Saxon Minister of Public Worship he carried out the plan he had cherished for a long time. He presented the Russian Minister in Dresden with a letter, in which he offered to go to the East, commissioned by the Tsar Alexander II, in search of old Greek and oriental manuscripts, particularly those of value to sacred literature. Any treasures thus acquired should belong to the Tsar. He naturally emphasized the importance of such a mission, not only in the interest of science, but for the whole Christian Church.

The Russian Minister of Culture, v. Noroff, was a highly educated man, and, knowing the East, he immediately saw the importance of the undertaking. The idea that the honour of such discoveries, as well as any valuable handwritings thus acquired should belong to Russia, also attracted him. From the very beginning, therefore, he interested himself in Tischendorf's proposal. When he came to Germany he even went to Leipzig to discuss the matter. He actually suggested, provided he could get off, that he should personally accompany the traveller, at least on the visit to the famous Monastery of the Holy Mount of Athos in Macedonia. The Imperial Academy in St. Petersburg, when asked for an opinion, expressed itself as wholly in favour.

The Oasis of the Wadi Feiran.

(See p. 42)

The Imperial Royal family was now drawn into the general interest. In particular the Grand Duke Konstantine, brother of the Tsar, was quite enthusiastic about the idea, that the undertaking would not only do great things for science and the Church, but would bring Russia any discovered handwritings as its property, and immense prestige besides. The two empresses, Empress Marie and the Empress Mother, also interested themselves in the plan. And at last the whole thing was brought to the most important person, to the Tsar himself. The Minister of Culture gave him a careful explanation, and the result was that Tischendorf was commissioned to undertake his journey as an emissary of the Tsar of Russia.

From now on things moved quickly. The Imperial Russian Minister in Dresden, Prince Wolkowsky, one day invited Tischendorf to visit him, and laid into his hand not only the necessary money for the journey, but a generous sum in Russian gold besides, in view of the expected purchases of old manuscripts. The Tsar herewith showed his faith in Tischendorf. He did not only give him all that was necessary for the expensive journey and expedition by camel through the desert of Sinai, as well as money enough for the purchases he might have to make,

E

but Tischendorf did not even have to give him a receipt. In fact, a receipt was expressly refused, while he was given a free hand as regards the execution of the undertaking. Neither verbally nor in writing were any conditions imposed upon him.

Thus, early in January, 1859, Tischendorf left Leipzig and sailed for Egypt. He stopped nowhere, neither in Alexandria nor in Cairo. Sinai drew him too powerfully. It was very doubtful whether he would still find those 86 pages which he had left behind. But even if these were lost to him, he knew how many other manuscripts, even though smaller and less precious, were still there. These too, were valuable, and to save them for science made the journey well worth while. These he wanted to purchase, and if this was impossible, he would at least copy them carefully, so that everyone might know their contents.

At the end of January, 1859, for the third time in fifteen years, he stepped into the quiet rooms of the St. Catharine Monastery. He was welcomed with joyful cries by the monks, and particularly by the old librarian Kyrillos, who had befriended him since 1844. The Russian Government had written to the Abbot advising him of the arrival of the Tsar's emissary, and had highly recommended him. The Abbot now received him with the words: ' I wish and hope that you may succeed in finding new light and new supports for Divine Truth.'

And now once more he began his thorough searchings in the poor library room, so well known to him. He naturally searched first and foremost for those 86 parchment pages, which fifteen years before he had held in his hand, having saved them from being burned. They had, however, vanished, and remained so. Not a soul in the whole monastery knew anything more about them, not even Kyrillos. Tischendorf therefore abandoned all hope of ever finding them. Amongst the other manuscripts, however, he found some valuable things, which he was able to purchase. He proposed adding these to the collections which he felt sure he would make during his intended long journey to the monasteries of the East. The real purpose of his third journey to Sinai remained unaccomplished, however, though outside of Sinai a big task still awaited him.

After a week he had finished everything and prepared to leave. He had ordered his Bedouins and camels for February 7, and was going to take his final farewell from the Holy Mountain. He was now forty-five years of age. A little later he would not be able to attempt the exertions of a journey through the desert, nor would he have anything further to look for. It was therefore also to take farewell that he went to the most noteworthy places in the vicinity before his departure. Two days before, he climbed once more to the summit of the Mount of Moses, and looked sadly out over the lonely, rocky and beautiful mountains. On the last day he made an excursion, together with the young steward of the monastery, an Athenian, to the Plain of Sebaje, on which, according to the monks, the Children of Israel stood when the Law was given to them from the Moses Mountain, which rose above them in rugged grandeur. With emotion he looked up once more to the colourful mountain giants, which he had learned to love during the past fifteen years. On the way back he talked to the young monk, who had been much impressed by the beautiful new editions of the Greek New Testament which Tischendorf had brought to the monastery as a present. And so it happened that the conversation turned around the fact that Tischendorf saw his life's work in the editing of the Greek text of the Bible. The Athenian seemed to appreciate that such an undertaking was indeed a life's work.

It was dusk before the two men returned to the monastery. The sun had already set behind the colossal rocks of Sinai, only the opposite eastern mountain top flamed in the ruddy glow of the sinking sun. Tischendorf wanted to take leave of his friendly companion and go to his own room. But the monk invited him to come over to his cell and to take some refreshments after the tiring walk. Tischendorf gladly accepted the invitation. He sat down by the modest table and gratefully took what the young Athenian handed him. While doing so the young man, animated by the conversation they had had by the road about the Greek Holy Scriptures, said : ' I also have a Greek Old Testament here in my cell. I will show it to you.' With that he rose, went into a corner of his cell and brought out a manuscript of unusual size, wrapped in a red cloth, which he laid in front of his guest on the table.

Tischendorf undid the knotted cloth and saw quite a big bundle of large parchment sheets. Pale with excitement, he could hardly believe his eyes. What did he see? The grand uncial characters, divided into four columns, of the precious Codex, of which he had taken 43 pages to Leipzig with him, and 86 of which he had left behind! There was no doubt about it. Every letter that he saw tallied exactly with those on the other sheets. A cold shiver ran through him. There before him lay what he had searched for through so many years with a burning desire, and which had finally occupied his mind, day and night, the precious remnant of those parchment pages, which he had once removed from the fateful basket.

But even more than that! When he looked more closely he found that there were not only 86 pages, but many, many more! There was quite a large bundle of sheets and as he rapidly glanced through them he saw that something far more valuable than just the missing sheets had come to light. He had before him what all his life had been the height of his dreams, the whole of the New Testament, from the Gospel of St. Matthew to the Revelation of St. John! He felt as if he were in a dream, for, among the books of the New Testament there lay also the Epistle of Barnabas, which for centuries had been lost. This epistle had during the first few centuries been regarded by the Christian churches as belonging to the New Testament, but it had finally been left out through a decision of the Synods.

Several other monks, including the old librarian Kyrillos, had entered the cell. They were silent witnesses of their guest's amazement. Tischendorf, however, held on to himself. He mastered his inner excitement, so as not to spoil the whole thing by showing over-much pleasure. He asked permission to take the manuscript to his room, to study it more closely. The permission was gladly granted. He wrapped the bundle into the red cloth again and carried his priceless burden across courtyards and up flights of stairs into his own room, the approach to which is shown in our illustration facing page 80.

Only when alone there, that evening about eight o'clock, could he allow himself to give way to the overwhelming effect which his discovery had had on him, a discovery which far surpassed all his wildest dreams and hopes. The first thing he did, however, was to go down on his knees and give thanks to God, who, as by a miracle, had led him suddenly to the fulfilment of his life's ambition. Only then did he begin studying the ancient manuscript which lay on the table before him. As he turned one sheet after another, how many new surprises! At the top of one sheet of parchment there stood as a heading, in faded old-fashioned characters: 'The Shepherd'. Oh yes, he had known this 'Shepherd' by name for a long while, but to-day for the first time in many centuries 'The Shepherd', written by Hermas, was seen by expert eyes. It was the other lost writing, which before the middle of the fourth century had in many churches been included in the New Testament. Thus in one stroke two lost manuscripts, which had been unsuccessfully searched for, had been found again. The first part of the epistle of Barnabas had up till then been known only in a rather poor Latin translation—the Hermas writing had long since been given up as lost for ever. But even more important than the rediscovery of these two epistles, which a later church had rejected as not being apostolic, was the fact that here was the whole of the New Testament, without any gaps, set down in an ancient manuscript. What an advantage over all other old manuscripts, even the most famous! Even the *Codex Vaticanus*, the most valuable of the hitherto known handwritings, as well as the *Codex Alexandrinus*, had large gaps. But not only the New Testament was contained in these sheets before him. No, here lay not only the 86 missing pages of the Old Testament, but 112 others as well, so that the Old Testament was also complete in this manuscript, every page of which was worth a fortune.

It was late. The candle lit the room but dimly, and at the same time gave off a little warmth in the cold place—that morning they had actually had some ice in the monastery—but owing to the riches which had fallen into his hand, Tischendorf could not sleep. In particular the long-lost epistle of Barnabas left him no peace.

ΑΡΧΗΤΟΥΕΥΑΓΓΕΛΙ
ΟΥΙ͞Υ Χ͞Υ Κ͞Α͞Θ͞Υ͞Θ͞ΥΘΩСΓΕ
ΓΡΑΠΤΑΙΕΝΤΩΗΑ
Ϊ ΑΤΩΠΡΟΦΗΤΗ
Ϊ ΔΟΥΕΓΩΑΠΟСΤΕ
ΛΩΤΟΝΑΓΓΕΛΟΝΜογ
ΠΡΟΠΡΟСΩΠΟΥСΟΥ
ΟСΚΑΤΑСΚΕΥΑСΕΙ

ΤΗΝΟΔΟΝСΟΥ
ΦΩΝΗΒΟΩΝΤΟСΕ͞
ΤΗΕΡΗΜΩΕΤΟΙΜΑ
СΑΤΕΤΗΝΟΔΟΝΚ͞Υ
ΕΥΘΙΑСΠΟΙΕΙΤΕΤΑС
ΤΡΙΒΟΥСΑΥΤΟΥΚΑΪΕ
ΓΕΝΕΤΟΙΩΑΝΝΗС
ΟΒΑΠΤΙΖΩΝΕΝΤΗ

St. Mark 1, 1-4

ω
ΚΑΙΕΓΕΝΕΤΟΕΝΕΚΕΙ
ΝΑΙΣΤΑΙΣΗΜΕΡΑΙC
ΗΛΘΕΝΙΣΑΠΟΝΑΖΑ
ΡΕΤΤΗΣΓΑΛΙΛΑΙΑC
ΚΑΙΕΒΑΠΤΙΣΘΗΕΙC
ΤΟΝΙΟΡΔΑΝΗΝΥΠΟ
ΙΩΑΝΝΟΥΚΑΙΕΥΘΥC
ΑΝΑΒΕΝΩΝΕΚΤΟΥ
ΥΔΑΤΟΣΕΙΔΕΝΣΧΙ
ΖΟΜΕΝΟΥΣΤΟΥC
ΟΥΝΟΥΣΚΑΙΤΟΠΝΑ
ΩΣΠΕΡΙΣΤΕΡΑΝΚΑ
ΤΑΒΑΙΝΟΝΚΑΙΜΕ
ΝΟΝΕΠΑΥΤΟΝ
ΚΑΙΦΩΝΗΕΚΤΩ

St. Mark 1, 9-11.

Codex Sinaiticus.

In spite of the darkness and the cold, he immediately began, right on into the small hours of the morning, to copy it out.

So much was certain; if he did not succeed in buying this treasure and taking it away with him, then he must carefully copy the whole manuscript from beginning to end to be able to publish it. Only in this way at least could the contents be saved. He believed he could accomplish this task in a few years. The famous Vatican manuscript was known for three centuries before the general desire for its publication was fulfilled. In this case it was to be different. If it lay in his power, he hoped to make this new discovery available to everyone in as many years.

Hardly had the first rays of the rising sun lit up the western peaks of Sinai, when Tischendorf sent for the young steward. Out of his great wealth he offered him two generous gifts, one for the monastery and one for himself, if he would help him in trying to take this manuscript as a gift to the Tsar of Russia. He could only admire the monk when he refused the money, saying: ' If these pages are as valuable as that, then they belong to the monastery.' On the other hand he agreed to allow Tischendorf to copy the manuscript, and the other Fathers of Mount Sinai had no objections.

The carrying out of this idea was, however, not so easy. A correct copy would at best take several months. Tischendorf, however, had no equipment. He had enough of everything only for a stay of eight days. He therefore asked permission to take the Codex to Cairo, where, in the filial monastery of the Fathers of Sinai, it would be as safe as here. There were good lodgings in Cairo, and he could there buy anything he needed. With this, too, the Fathers and Brothers of the Monastery agreed, with the exception of the Skevophylax Vitalios, the keeper of the altar plate, out of whose store the manuscript had found its way into the steward's cell. During these discussions Tischendorf also discovered how it happened that instead of 86 sheets there were now so many more. Shortly after his departure from the Monastery in 1844 someone had found the rest of the manuscript in another room of the monastery, in all 260 sheets. As the departed guest had declared the sheets found in the waste-paper basket to be so valuable, they had started to search, and had found the major portion of the Codex under the dust among the church furniture in the store-room of the Skevophylax. As Vitalios had the 260 sheets, they had given him the 86 sheets which hitherto had been in Kyrillos' keeping, to make the Codex complete. The whole manuscript, however, had in the meantime been forgotten by the ignorant monks, so that when Tischendorf came the second time, they were quite honest when they said they knew nothing about it. Now, however, as the stranger once more declared them to be so precious, Vitalios, as keeper of the Church treasure, preferred to keep the Codex in the Monastery, rather than let it go to Cairo.

If the monks had been unanimous, Tischendorf could without further trouble have taken the manuscript to Cairo. As this was not the case, however, only the Abbot could decide, and he unfortunately was away. The Archbishop of the Sinai Order had died at the age of ninety, and all the abbots of the monasteries belonging to the Order had collected in Cairo. From there they were going to travel to Constantinople, to the residence of the Œcumenical Patriarch, for the new election. The previous election, though unanimous, had been contested by the unfriendly Patriarch of Jerusalem, who would have had to consecrate the new archbishop. It was for this reason that the abbots had now to undertake the journey to Constantinople to have a re-election. As Tischendorf could achieve nothing with the monks only, he decided to ride to Cairo as quickly as possible, in the hope of catching the Abbot, who doubtless would give his consent, before he left for Constantinople.

On February 7, the Bedouin Sheik Nasser, whom Tischendorf had ordered, camped with his men and his camels beneath the walls of the monastery, to take Tischendorf back to Egypt. The great winds, which for the last few days and nights had swept around the monastery and the mighty hills, had dropped that morning. The cloudless blue sky promised a good journey. High above the monastery the Russian flag had been hoisted, in honour of the Tsar's emissary. From the flat monastery roof a salute was fired, the sound of which came back in a thousand echoes from the mountains of Sinai. Several of the monks, including the old Kyrillos and the steward, would not hear of being denied the pleasure of escorting Tischendorf as far as the Plain of Raha. Much moved, and with great gratitude, Tischendorf bade them farewell for the third and last time. In a hurried march he covered the desert road to Suez in seven days.

On February 13 he arrived in Cairo. The next morning he appeared in the Monastery of the Fathers of Sinai, and to his great pleasure found the Abbot still there. He mentioned his request, which was supported by a very warm note from Kyrillos and the steward. Agathangelos, the chief of the Abbots present, was very obliging. He placed the whole question before the assembled Fathers; after a short consultation they all agreed that the manuscript be brought to the monastery in Cairo.

A sheik was sent to Sinai to fetch the manuscript. Tischendorf promised him a large 'baksheesh' if he carried out the commission with all speed. The man sped through the desert on a racing camel, and accomplished the seemingly impossible. In twelve days, on February 23, he once more dismounted from his camel in front of the Cairo monastery. Never was a more precious load carried on the back of a camel through the lonely mountains and valleys of the Sinai desert. Immediately next morning the venerable Agathangelos appeared at the hotel with his locum, and showed Tischendorf the valuable parcel brought by camel post. At the Russian Consulate an agreement was signed, by which Tischendorf was permitted to take eight pages of the manuscript at a time from the monastery to his lodgings, there to copy them.

8

THE FURTHER FATE OF THE *CODEX SINAITICUS*

TISCHENDORF had only been in Cairo a few days when from another quarter an attempt was made on the Codex. The discovery was at first to be kept a secret. But as the result of confidential information, an Englishman had heard of it. He immediately appeared at the Cairo monastery and succeeded in getting the unsuspecting Fathers to let him see the Codex, whereupon he offered them a big price for it.

But the honest monks refused. The Abbot Agathangelos who related the happening to the alarmed Tischendorf, said: ' We would rather give the manuscript to our powerful fellow-believer, the Tsar Alexander II, as a present, than sell it for English money.' This occurrence, however, decided Tischendorf. He made up his mind to publish the first news of his lucky discovery straight away, so as to avoid the possibility of the other giving himself out as being the discoverer. Thus the first news of the finding of the

Codex in the old Monastery of Sinai got into the
European newspapers and created a sensation
amongst the people who could estimate its value.

In the meantime, the tremendous work of
copying the Codex was being undertaken in
Cairo, in spite of the summer heat of the Nile
country. For two months Tischendorf sat in his
hotel of the Pyramids, under whose windows the
busy and colourful life of the old town of the
Caliphs passed by. But he seldom took the time
to look out upon it. He worked and worked.
He could not accomplish the great task by himself. He therefore got two reliable German
countrymen who knew Greek, to help him, one a
doctor and the other a chemist. They wrote and
wrote incessantly. It was necessary to copy the
110,000 lines of the Sinai Bible most carefully.
Tischendorf himself could not give much time to
the actual copying. To him fell the task of
scrupulously examining all that the other two had
written. This was particularly important as it
concerned not only a straightforward text, but
all the innumerable corrections and supposed
improvements which had been added by a
later hand to the original manuscript. On
some of these 346 pages there were more than
a hundred such corrections, which in all totalled
more than twelve thousand. One can well

imagine, therefore, what an immense task was Tischendorf's, as the responsible person. Everything that the others had written he had to compare letter by letter with the original, and put right even the smallest mistake, either in the text or in the minutely written corrections.

In the middle of this work a new difficulty arose. The Fathers and Elders of the Order of Sinai had been promised that the desired ratification of the election, and the consecration of their new Archbishop, would take place very shortly, after which nothing stood in the way of the presentation of the manuscript to the Tsar of Russia. Then the message came that the unfriendly patriarch of Jerusalem, who, according to the rules of the Order, could alone undertake the consecration, once more objected, and questioned the validity of the election. Owing to this, even the presentation to the Tsar became doubtful. The heads of the Sinai monasteries therefore begged Tischendorf, as the Tsar's envoy, to help them.

In his own interest he could not refuse them. He had gathered from the newspapers that the Grand Duke Konstantine, whom he knew from St. Petersburg, where the former had assisted him so kindly with the execution of his plans, was just now going to visit Jerusalem with a large retinue.

The gallery leading to Tischendorf's
room in the monastery.

(See p. 71)

Tischendorf quickly made up his mind to interrupt his work and travel to Jerusalem, in the hope
of enlisting the powerful intervention of the Grand
Duke. He went to Alexandria, to sail from there
to Palestine, but he looked out unsuccessfully for
a ship that might be sailing for Jaffa. There
were, however, three other travellers besides
himself whose destination was Jaffa, a Russian
general, a Prussian lieutenant of a Hussar
regiment, and an American civilian. The
Turkish shipping company, therefore, for a
goodly sum, and also in the expectation that the
opportunity thus offered might attract other
travellers, put a special steamer at their disposal.

At last, on the morning of May 5, Tischendorf
sailed out to sea, making for the coast of the Holy
Land. Next day he landed at Jaffa. About
noon he saw on the horizon out at sea two frigates,
coming from the north. Immediately the flags
were hoisted on the Russian and other consulates,
a sign that the sighted ships were bringing the
eminent guest. That same evening, after the
Grand Duke had landed, the Russian Consul
presented him with a letter which Tischendorf
had sent ahead, announcing the lucky find of
Sinai. The Grand Duke welcomed this information with real joy, and ordered that the explorer,
who was waiting in quarantine, be liberated from

there, and accompany his procession to Jerusalem
next day, on one of his own horses.   On the way,
in the delightful valley of Kulonje, the opportunity presented itself for Tischendorf to greet the
Grand Duke, who, together with the Grand
Duchess, received him in a most friendly way.
One of the Grand Duke's first questions was, how
the end of the Gospel according to St. Mark was
worded in the Sinai Bible, for it was given in so
many different versions in the old manuscripts,
that up to that day no one had been able to
ascertain the correct ending.   This question
alone was proof that the Grand Duke had understanding of the importance of the Sinai discovery.

During a detailed report on this situation which
followed later in Jerusalem, it was not difficult to
get the Grand Duke's promise that the Russian
Government would interest itself in the whole
matter; that it would use its influence with the
Turkish Government and the obstinate Patriarch,
with a view to bringing to a happy close the
disputed election, and make the presentation of
the old manuscript to the Russian Tsar possible.

In Constantinople the matter could not be
arranged so quickly however.   It might take
months before everything was settled. Tischendorf
did not want to let this time go by in idleness.   He
therefore decided to use it for his other journeys

of discovery in the East. He first went to Asia
Minor. In Smyrna in particular he did not
search in vain, for he there found a complete
Uncial-Manuscript of the four gospels of the ninth
century. He then embarked on a sailing ship,
which carried him across the ocean to the Island
of Patmos, the island known to all readers as
the place where the Apostle John lived in exile,
and where, on a memorable Sunday, he received
the Revelation.

From Patmos Tischendorf wrote to his wife in
Leipzig:

'From Smyrna I rode to Scala Nuova, where
I embarked for here. The sea was rough,
which made the crossing anything but pleasant.
I was all the more grateful when, at 7 o'clock
in the evening, I set foot on the lonely, rocky,
seagirt island, so well known to all Christendom.
At 8 o'clock I arrived, on foot, at the top of the
hill, from where the monastery looks out over
the sea like a mighty Acropolis. I stayed in
the monastery all the week, and was treated
with deference, especially as they saw in me the
envoy of the Tsar. The professor there, who had
lived in Leipzig for six years, was kindness
itself. The Abbot even said yesterday: " If a
king had come, it would not have pleased me

as much as your visit," for he has entrusted me with some requests which the monastery has to the Turks, and which he hopes I will sponsor in St. Petersburg. In the library of the monastery I saw several excellent manuscripts. The Bishop has even given me some valuable manuscripts which I am bringing back with me, as the rich fruits of my journey. To-day, Saturday, the quiet of the Sabbath has returned to the sea, which on my arrival was so rough. How one's thoughts go back over centuries to that distant Sunday when the apostle, in the loneliness of this rocky coast, was removed in spirit and received his Revelation from Heaven, while about him was the rushing sound of the waves.'

After three months of successful journeys Tischendorf returned to Egypt at the end of July. There he hoped to receive the message that, thanks to the intervention of the Russian Government, all the obstacles which stood in the way of the presentation of the Codex, had been removed. Unfortunately, however, this hope was vain. Still the truculent Patriarch refused to acknowledge the unanimous election, and to ordain the new archbishop of the Order of Sinai. The Fathers were deeply discouraged. The whole

life of the Order was disorganized, and there
was no saying if and when this would change.
They saw but one way out: Tischendorf, the
envoy of the most powerful emperor, was in
their midst and must help. Earnestly they begged
of him.

Tischendorf therefore decided that he must go
to Constantinople to push on the matter there, at
the seat of the Sultan and the Russian Ambassador. Once again he had to interrupt his work
in Cairo. A fortnight later, on August 10, he
left Egypt once more, and on the 17th of the
month he landed at Stambul. At the Russian
Embassy he was received with greatest attention
and amiability, as the Tsar's envoy. The ambassador, Prince Lobanow, immediately invited him
to stay in the summer palace of the Embassy
in Bujukdere for the duration of his visit. It was
magnificently furnished and was situated with a
view of the delightful bays of the Bosphorus.
The Ambassador, a highly educated diplomat
full of interest for art and science, energetically
sponsored the matter concerning the Fathers of
Sinai. He knew that in doing so he was acting
in a way which his Imperial Master would
approve. The Grand Vizier and the Turkish
ministers, in view of this authoritative interces-
sion, were ready to agree to anything. But

even then things did not move as quickly as Tischendorf had hoped.   Not only was ' Jawash, Jawash ' (to-morrow, to-morrow) the general watchword in Turkey, but the Sublime Porte, so as to avoid a controversy in the whole of the Greek Church, had in fact to approach the matter very carefully.

One week after another slipped by, and finally, in spite of the grand life on the beautiful banks of the Bosphorus, Tischendorf grew restive.   Day and night his thoughts kept reverting to his Codex in Cairo.   Then at last the Ambassador suggested a possible way out of the difficulties.   In the name of the Tsar he wrote a letter to the monastery of Sinai, in which he promised the monastery the Tsar's help in its difficulties, but at the same time suggested that the old manuscript be lent to Tischendorf for the time being, for him to take to St. Petersburg.   He also undertook, in the name of the Tsar, to guarantee the safe return of the manuscript to the monastery, should the suggested presentation not materialize.

With this letter, after a five weeks' stay, Tischendorf once more embarked and returned to Cairo on September 27.   The governing bodies of the monasteries received him with great pleasure. Through their representatives in Constantinople they had heard how emphatically the Ambassador had defended their rights. They did not doubt that, thanks to this help, they would achieve their aim. That it should just be Tischendorf who had procured this help for them, filled them with warmest gratitude towards him.

All the more willingly did they accept the Ambassador's suggestion. A monastery convention was called, and soon the venerable Agathangelos informed Tischendorf that Prince Lobanow's suggestion had been accepted unanimously. The confidence of the Fathers of Mount Sinai was later well rewarded, for the Russian Ambassador succeeded in having all their wishes fulfilled.

And now, after so much trouble and long journeys, everything had been accomplished that Tischendorf had hoped for. On September 28 the manuscript was handed over to him, on his express wish, in the same red cloth in which the steward of the St. Catharine Monastery had first brought it to him on February 4. Overjoyed, he carried the treasure into the hotel, or rather, he got the monastery servants to carry it there for him, for the total number of parchment sheets was a pretty heavy load. Even though the presentation to the Tsar had not yet taken place, the most important thing had been achieved; he could take the manuscript to Europe with him and could there have it copied, duplicated, and published.   By these means everything had been safeguarded for science.

On October 9, after having travelled about to many different places in the East, he once more set out for Europe.   After he had landed in Trieste he was tempted to travel on as quickly as possible.   Nevertheless, he stopped in Vienna to show his valuable find to the Emperor Franz Joseph, who had earlier shown him his great interest in the matter.   He was received at the Hofburg with all ceremony, and the Emperor examined with amazement this document from the first century of the Christian Church.   The next person to see the Codex was Tischendorf's own sovereign, King John of Saxony, who received him in the palace at Dresden, and honoured him in diverse ways.   And then Tischendorf had to call at the Russian Legation there, where he had received the Tsar's commission.   Prince Wolkowsky was delighted that everything had succeeded so well, beyond all hopes and expectations.   He then organized an exhibition in the Legation to which a lot of people of all classes came, to see the Codex which had quickly become famous.

From Dresden Tischendorf went to Leipzig, and from there, after a short reunion with his wife and children, he travelled without further

The Gebel Katherina.

(See p. 46)

delay to St. Petersburg, where he arrived in the middle of November.

The Tsar and the Tsarina received him with great joy and heartiest congratulations in the summer palace of Tsarskoje-Selo, and together with the Grand Duke and the whole Court, inspected the Codex, which was still wrapped in the red cloth in which it was discovered eight months previously at the foot of the Holy Mountain. The inspection took place in the 'Chinese Room' in the palace. Not only the *Codex Sinaiticus*, as the great centrepiece, was laid out there, but also the entire collection of all the other manuscripts which the lucky discoverer had brought back from the East. Amongst them also were the twelve palimpsests, which created great interest, with their old, pale characters, that had been nearly washed off several centuries before. The Tsar was delighted at the thought that in future these treasures would be Russian property. To the highest dignitaries of the Russian Church, the Holy Synod, Tischendorf showed the Codex at a later date. After this, according to a wish expressed by the Tsar, an exhibition was arranged in the Imperial Public Library of all the manuscripts and antiquities. This exhibition was visited not only by the nobility, but by countless men and women of the people.

In the whole of Europe the strange discovery on Mount Sinai was discussed in all the newspapers and in all quarters. It sounded like a fairy tale, that in the far away monastery in the desert such a treasure should have been found after being forgotten for many hundreds of years, and that it should have been saved at the last moment from being destroyed by fire. Everyone commended the man whose energy and untiring perseverance had achieved this. Nearly all the European courts showered so many orders and distinctions upon him that they could never have found room on one man's chest.

9

THE PUBLICATION OF THE *CODEX SINAITICUS*

THE next task to be taken in hand was the publication of the old Bible-Manuscript, which, by the Grace of God, through the storms of centuries, had yet been preserved to this day, and had once more been brought to light. To enable him to devote himself entirely to the work, Tischendorf received an honorary appointment to St. Petersburg, which also financially placed him in a much better position than in his post as University Professor in Leipzig. But it did not even need the efforts of the Saxon Government to keep him at home: in this direction he himself did not aspire to higher things. He therefore declined, but naturally declared himself willing to crown his work by supervising the publication in Leipzig, in the name of the Russian Emperor. Several journeys to St. Petersburg were necessary so as to arrange with the Russian Government what sort of lines the publication was to take.

The journeys, mostly undertaken in the winter,

were not as comfortable as in these days, when one can get into a heated through carriage or sleeper in Berlin and remain comfortably seated until one reaches St. Petersburg. From Königsberg one had first of all to travel east by mail coach. In Russia one traversed tracts covered in snow in a sledge, through towering snowdrifts. Repeatedly one got stuck in the snow, and the sledge or carriage threatened to overturn. Everyone had to get out, until a way had been cut through. Once Tischendorf had to buy his own sledge, to make headway. And when the lonely sledge sped over the silent, white surface, as often as not it was surrounded by hungry wolves, who followed the vehicle with ravenous howls. It was often an adventurous journey. But finally he would reach the Russian railway, which would carry him to St. Petersburg without further dangers, though often with a severe cold in the head.

In St. Petersburg everyone agreed with Tischendorf that the exterior of the book must in some way reflect the value of the unique document. Also, as the publication was undertaken in the name and by order of the Emperor, it must in every way be a particularly fine edition. With these instructions he returned to his work in Leipzig.

At first Tischendorf was in doubt as to the method of reproduction. From several quarters a photographic copy was suggested, and the Tsar was quite willing to defray the cost of M.300,000. In spite of this, Tischendorf decided against the photographic process. There were several pages where not only the characters were much faded, but which contained extensive corrections and eradications, often one over the other, so that it seemed very doubtful whether a photograph would be successful. Besides this, to produce 700 photographic plates with, in all, about 210,000 prints, which would be necessary for the suggested 300 copies, would take a long time. And finally there were those who doubted the durability of photographs. Tischendorf therefore decided to photograph only a part of the most interesting pages for special purposes, and to reproduce the whole manuscript by means of printing. In this way the publication would also be hastened. This speeding up was in the first place in the interest of science, for rather naturally amongst the interested circles one was looking forward to this work with the greatest curiosity. Besides this, however, it so happened that in the autumn of 1862 the thousand years Jubilee of the Russian monarchy was impending, for the celebration of which the Emperor wanted to see the

Codex published. Up to that date, however, there were now only twenty-seven months, a very short time for such a gigantic undertaking. The reader may think that just over two years should be ample time for the printing of such a book. He will, however, soon see from the following descriptions that it was not so in this case.

There now followed more than two years during which Tischendorf sat day after day working on this Codex, which had been written thirteen centuries before. He thus got to know the Codex thoroughly, not only from the inside, but also from the outside. Those large pages, after all, consisted of parchment, that is to say, of the untanned skins of animals, which had been cleaned, freed of the hair, pickled with lime and then smoothed. He soon learned to distinguish whether the parchment pages consisted of the skins of gazelles or of other animals. The parchments varied accordingly, in colour, texture, and flexibility. For the legibility of the writing it also mattered whether the writer had written on the hair or the flesh side of the smoothed skin.

Let us look over his shoulder and see him working on, and studying his beloved Codex. He is sitting at his writing table.[1]

[1] This table now stands in my wife's room. She was born shortly after the great discovery at the St. Catharine Monastery, and in memory thereof was given the name of Catharine.

The reader would be very astonished if he could see the characters of that manuscript. It all looks quite different from our printed books of to-day. First of all, the difference between the small and the capital letters does not exist. What we see there are only large, so-called uncial letters. And there is something else lacking, which in our present-day Bibles we take entirely for granted. We cannot imagine any Bible without its books divided into chapters and verses, so that we can see at a glance what part we have before us. There is none of this in the *Codex Sinaiticus*. Nowhere in the continuous writing is there a paragraph. We are also used to having the sentences punctuated by commas, points and question marks, which all help to make the sense clearer to us. The words are divided from one another by spaces, which assist the reader even more than the difference between the large and small letters.

As in all other manuscripts of that time, so also in the *Codex Sinaiticus*, all this does not exist. The dividing into chapters was first instituted by Cardinal Hugo a Santo Caro in the year 1250. Verses came into existence after Luther's time, about the year 1551, and were first introduced by the printer Robert Stephanus of Paris. He himself printed and published a New Testament, and on his own initiative divided the chapters into verses, thus establishing the custom for all time. Unfortunately the division into chapters and verses is often both clumsy and confusing, so that in many cases it obscures the sense. None of all these divisions, however, are to be found in the *Codex Sinaiticus*. There are no chapters, no verses, no spaces between the words, and no difference between large and small letters. From beginning to end of each Book there are only capital letters which, without space or interruption, run on line after line.

The large sized sheets of parchment contain the writing in four columns, as the reader can see from the two illustrations[1] which are a faithful copy of the *Codex Sinaiticus*. They have been taken from the first chapter of the Gospel according to St. Mark. On writing of this kind Tischendorf had to work for a long time, to prepare the great work for print.

The printing, however, could not be commenced immediately, for the letters with which one usually prints books, were all useless on this occasion. As every letter had to resemble the original exactly, new letters had to be made, such as were then unknown to the art of printing.

Tischendorf entrusted the well-known printing

[1] See illustrations facing pp. 72 and 73.

The entrance to the monastery and
the windlass.

(See p. 43)

firm of Giesecke and Devrient in Leipzig with this difficult task. The letters of the manuscript were first photographed. From these photographs the dies were cut, which formed the characters of the continuous text. This first type, however, was not yet sufficient. On almost every page of the original there were marginal notes, insertions, and footnotes, all of which showed a considerably smaller and different kind of alphabet. These corrections and the inserted writings had, in the finished publication, to appear in exactly the same place and form. It was therefore necessary to photograph this small writing as well, and cut an identical alphabet, letter for letter. But even this did not suffice. A third and still smaller alphabet had to correspond with the letters of about 16,000 corrections and additions in the smallest possible type. The reader can scarcely imagine what a strain this was on Tischendorf's head and eyes. The characters were not clear cut and well defined as in a printed book, but it was often a case of faded letters, which fifteen hundred years before had been altered by eradications and various signs.

During these comprehensive preparations on the part of Giesecke and Devrient, Tischendorf had had a copperplate paper specially made by the well-known factory of Ferdinand Flinsch in

Leipzig. This paper was of considerable size, and besides being handsome and durable, had to resemble the parchment of the manuscript as closely as possible. Only twenty copies were printed on real parchment, and were intended for royal recipients.

In June 1860 the printing could at last begin, and at the beginning of July Tischendorf saw with emotion the first finished pages lying on his table. During the progress of the printing several improvements were made for the purpose of making a still more accurate imitation of the manuscript. On minute examination of the individual letters, it became evident that the Codex was not written by one and the same hand. The Codex probably originated in Alexandria, where the most skilful and famous calligraphists of that distant century lived, and the whole task was evidently divided among several of these men. It is true that the writing of the Codex was so marvellously regular that every layman would have sworn that it had all come from the same hand. But Tischendorf, the foremost palaeographer of his time, with his sharp eyes, distinguished four different hands, of which each had some peculiarity of its own. He therefore had a number of complementary letters cut. In this way the one letter Omega alone finally had seven variations. The smallest line had to correspond exactly with the original, including all its minute irregularities. One of the most tedious and wearisome things was that the spaces between the letters which the old calligraphists had placed unevenly, were to be exactly copied. One can hardly imagine how much hard work this entailed. In each case Tischendorf had to prescribe the exact distances to the compositor, and then take particular note of them when proof reading. This spacing between the letters was achieved by slipping in the thinnest metal leaves between the type. Every single page contained, on an average, 1,200 such spaces, with more than 2,500 metal leaves. In proof reading, letter for letter had once more to be carefully compared with the original, in order to ascertain the number of metal leaves to be inserted. Thus, for instance, for the text of the New Testament alone, several hundred thousands of these metal leaves of varying sizes were measured, inserted and checked.

Through this unexpected increase of the work, the completion became almost impossible within so short a space of time. In order to complete the three volumes within two years it was a question of copying by hand, preparing, setting, correcting, revising and ultimately printing, no less than thirty-two columns with forty-eight lines each every week. In addition to this work, necessitating minute attention, many journeys were undertaken. Several visits to St. Petersburg became necessary. King William of Prussia also expressed a wish to see the Codex. For this reason Tischendorf travelled to Berlin, and the Codex was received with the greatest interest by the King and Queen, as well as by the Crown Prince and Crown Princess.

In spite of all difficulties, Tischendorf's indefatigable industry succeeded in accomplishing the task in time. Just after Easter, 1862, the printing of the three folio volumes, with twenty-two books of the Old Testament and twenty-nine books of the New Testament, and including the epistles of Barnabas and Hermas, was completed. The great achievement on the part of the printer, on whom such immense and unusual demands had been made, was beyond all praise. Everything corresponded exactly with the original, including the brown-coloured printer's ink. The red letters often occurring in the middle of the text, and the manifold little signs were faithfully reproduced.

A further gigantic piece of work of Tischendorf's was the scientific introduction and exposition of the Sinai Manuscript. It formed the fourth folio volume of the work. In it he had

given 15,000 explanations, most of which concerned the alterations which had been introduced
by the correctors into the ancient manuscript
between the fourth and ninth, and in the twelfth
century. Several thousand explanations concerned passages, the understanding of which was
particularly difficult, as the original writing had
been erased, re-written, and very often these
corrections once more eradicated and re-written
by still later correctors. It was necessary not only
to ascertain what was originally written and what
was added later, but it was also necessary to find
out which of the seven correctors was the author
of any particular passage.

As already mentioned, however, everything
had succeeded well, in spite of the shortness of
time, and Tischendorf could take the whole
completed work, with its three hundred reproduc-
tions of the ancient manuscript which he had
found on Sinai, to Russia, in time for the thousand
years Jubilee. On the day of his departure for St.
Petersburg, on October 6, 1862, thirty-one cases
with 1,232 folio volumes, with a total weight of
130 cwt., were despatched there. In the middle
of October he reached the Russian capital. At
Tsarkoje-Selo, on November 10, the Emperor and
Empress received, with the expression of their
warmest thanks, the first copies from his hands.

On its first page the work contained a dedication to the Tsar and Tsarina, in the following words: ' The Lord has ordained that, under the auspices of your Imperial Majesty, this treasure of an original Christian document be brought to Europe three years ago from a secluded corner of a monastery in the East.   Thanks to His infinite mercy, it was granted to me to accomplish this work of countless years within three years, and I now lay it at your Imperial Majesty's feet.   I do this having the joyful satisfaction of knowing that the great importance of this manuscript, which I so confidently foresaw, has been so marvellously confirmed.   There is no original document which can present more valid proofs of its ancient nobility. From the earliest Christian antiquity, venerable Fathers from the East and West appear as witnesses to the fact that the church of their day had before it the Word of God in similar documents.

' Thus this Christian relic from the time of the first Christian Emperor has lain like a holy treasure at the foot of the mountain, on whose summit Moses once saw the Glory of God and received from God's Hands the Tables of the Law.   But after being hidden for many centuries, it was destined to be laid into Your Majesty's hand, in order that, with its eloquent message of old Divine Truth, it be given to the entire Christian world.'

Of the 300 special copies of large size, 223 were sent to the best known libraries in the Christian world, as a present from the Russian Tsar. Naturally a copy of the magnificent work in four volumes went to the St. Catharine Monastery on Sinai, with a present of gold from the Emperor. One copy was also sent to the family Tischendorf. The remaining seventy-seven the Emperor presented to the discoverer Constantine von Tischendorf, with a view to selling them through a bookseller. They were therefore sent back from St. Petersburg to Leipzig, and were sold by Giesecke and Devrient at high prices.

Through the widespread distribution of this work, the text of the *Sinaiticus*, in the most faithful reproduction of the original, had become common property of Christianity. When, shortly afterwards, the long intended presentation of the Codex had been performed by a delegation from Sinai to the Emperor, the Codex found its place in the Public Library of the Russian capital.

Even if the original document should fall a prey to an evil chance—the danger lay near enough at the outbreak of the Russian Revolution and Bolshevik madness, in the year 1917— still the most valuable text of the New Testament has, through this publication, been preserved for all time.

10

THE IMPORTANCE OF THE SINAI MANUSCRIPT

THE reader will no doubt have been asking: How old then is the Sinai Manuscript? To this I must still answer: Unfortunately it does not carry its birth certificate on its parchment sheets. We are therefore dependent on the other signs which it bears. These are, however, so clear and unmistakable that its age can be determined pretty accurately.

First of all it is an established fact that Emperor Justinian in Constantinople founded the Sinai Monastery in the year 530. He had a special veneration for this sanctuary and was most eager to furnish it with everything which a prominent monastery should possess. One of the first essentials was, of course, a library, which must, above all, contain, besides the legends of the saints, a copy of the Holy Scriptures.

In Alexandria, situated so near the Peninsula of Sinai, there lived in the fourth century the most famous calligraphists of the day, who understood how to produce the books ordered with the greatest skill and uniformity. It is to be expected that the Emperor would wish to present to the Sinai Monastery a Bible written by these experts. And actually the excellent writing of the Codex has, among other signs, those that point to its Alexandrine origin.

These are, however, only suppositions. To make sure, one must consult the manuscript itself with regard to its age. One is here dependent on a minute examination of the historic signs and the nature of the writing. Palaeographers (experts on old manuscripts), as well as scholars of church history, can from this deduce such unmistakable proofs, that the age of the Sinai Manuscript cannot be subject to any doubt. This is, however, a matter for the expert, and is beyond the scope of this little book. We can be satisfied with the unanimous opinion of scholars.

The entire learned profession of research agreed with what Tischendorf, as the foremost master of palaeography of his time, established. In the dedication of his Codex, Tischendorf wrote these words: 'There is no original document of this kind which can present more valid proofs of its ancient nobility.'

The only Greek Manuscript which might be compared with the *Sinaiticus* as regards age is the *Codex Vaticanus*, which is in the possession of the Pope. The *Vaticanus* has, however, for a long time been acknowledged as dating from the fourth century. Both these manuscripts bear marks of a great age, such as exist in no other Bible handwritings. In these other early manuscripts which lie in Paris, Rome, London, Dublin and Wolfenbüttel for instance, the New Testament has already the division into chapters, which was introduced later. Only the *Sinaiticus* and the *Vaticanus* have the older form of writing, without chapters. Here everything is written straight on, and there is, from the beginning to the end of each book, not a single paragraph. Besides this, certain peculiarities are common to both. Nowhere at the beginning of the sentences are there any capital letters. Also such punctuation marks as commas, points, and question marks, are also entirely lacking. There are, however, signs in the *Sinaiticus* which prove that it is still older than the *Vaticanus*, for in the former the sequence of the books of the New Testament is the same as in the oldest known translation in Syrian. In the *Vaticanus*, on the other hand, the books are in the same order as in our present Bible. Added to this it would seem that, at the time of the writing of the *Sinaiticus*, the epistles of Barnabas and Hermas were still included in the New Testament. We know that the Churches of the second and third centuries were inclined to include these two, as well as the apostolic writings, in their Bible, proof of which we have from Clemence (died 220) and Origines (died 255). When, in the year 325, Eusebius compiled an index of those books of the New Testament which were generally or only partially acknowledged in the churches, he placed the epistles of Barnabas and Hermas among the latter. It was only at the church assemblies at Laodicea in 364, and at Carthage in 397, that they were finally excluded from the New Testament. There thus exist a great number of unmistakable signs of the great age of the manuscript, which are of the utmost importance to the scientists, but need not be enumerated here. It is sufficient to say that everything points with certainty to the fact that the *Codex Sinaiticus* was written before the middle of the fourth century, at the time of Eusebius, who died 340. That is an age which no other Greek book manuscript has.

But that is not all: the *Sinaiticus* points back to still earlier antiquity. It is closely related not only to the *Vaticanus*, but also to the oldest Latin translation of the Bible, the *Itala*. As this translation goes as far back as the second century, it is a guarantee that the text, as found in the *Sinaiticus*, was already in use in the second century, and, as the oldest Syrian gospel text expressly states,

widely known.   For the faithful preservation of
the text it was a good thing that the calligraphists
in Alexandria in the fourth century did not understand Greek, for they were therefore not tempted
to make corrections, such as many later copyists
did, with the best intentions but in ignorance.
From all of which it will be seen that, for the
restoration of the original text, as the apostles
wrote it, the Sinai Manuscript is more important
than any other.

The reader will doubtless ask: Have we then
no longer the original apostolic text in our New
Testament? In the main, certainly. But before
the invention of printing, all books had to be
written by hand. Thus the writings of the New
Testament could only be preserved by their text
being copied again and again, from the time of
the Apostles onward. As, however, copies were
made from copies, the text naturally ran the risk
of becoming faulty. The cause of this was often
carelessness, misunderstanding or ignorance on
the part of the writer, especially as the writing of
that time, as in the case of the *Sinaiticus*, had neither
spaces between the words nor any punctuation
marks; the letters followed one another without
any interruption. In many cases incorrectness
was also owing, not only to carelessness, but to
over zeal on the part of the writers, who endea-

voured to improve an expression, to complete a
story, or to correct supposed differences and
contradictions, without realizing that they were
thereby sinning against the Bible text. As the
libraries of the Christian world possess in all
several thousand original documents of the writings of the New Testament, and likewise a large
number of old Syrian, Coptic, Latin, and Gothic
translations, the rendering of the text varies so
considerably that only quite a few verses are in
complete accord with one another. Many a
verse has ten or more different versions, even if
these are chiefly of a linguistic rather than a
material nature.

I should not like the reader to imagine that he
can no longer quite trust his New Testament,
in which in the original text so many errors occur.
For there is not the least occasion for this. It is
only in a few passages that the disparities have
any real material importance.

In Mark xvi, for instance, we have not the real
ending which the evangelist had originally
written. As far as verse 8 all manuscripts agree,
but St. Mark himself did not write what is in our
New Testament from verse 9 to the end. It
was already known that this ending did not exist
in the hitherto oldest and most important
manuscript, the *Vaticanus*, and that also the most

eminent Christian Fathers of the Church of the fourth century testified that it did not then exist in the most accurate manuscripts. Through the discovery of the *Codex Sinaiticus*, the most ancient Greek manuscript, it was confirmed that here also the ending from verses 9-20, as known to us, was at that time not included in the Gospel of St. Mark, which therefore closed with verse 8. If now the reader opens his New Testament, he will find it recorded of the women who went to the sepulchre: ' And they went out quickly and fled from the sepulchre, for they trembled and were amazed; neither said they any thing to any man, for they were afraid.'

Now everyone will be under the impression that St. Mark cannot have concluded his Gospel in this way. What follows? That already very early the real ending, written by St. Mark himself, must, through some mischance, have been torn off or got lost in some way. The copyists too felt this, and with the best intentions endeavoured to add an ending which might be in accordance with the other Gospels, so that an obviously unfinished work should not fall into the hands of their readers. In this way there arose, in course of time, a number of endings with a different reading. The best known ending, which is already to be found in the old Latin translation of the *Itala*, is in our Luther Bible. This connection of circumstances, already suspected for some time, was made certain through the discovery of the *Sinaiticus*. For now the two oldest witnesses, the *Sinaiticus* and the *Vaticanus*, agree.

Another instance: In the first verse of the epistle to the Ephesians we read in our Bibles that it was addressed to the saints at Ephesus. But the word Ephesus is missing in the Codex, as in all other manuscripts. It has only been added by later copyists. It has, therefore, become clear, what had already been suspected from internal signs, that this epistle was not addressed to the Ephesians at all. Probably it was written by St. Paul during his imprisonment in Ephesus,[1] and cannot therefore have been addressed to Ephesus.

[1] It is an established fact that St. Paul wrote the Epistles to the Colossians and to the Ephesians from some imprisonment at the same time with the short letter to Philemon. Philemon lived in Colossæ, and his runaway slave Onesimus met St. Paul on his flight and was converted. It is not impossible that Onesimus came to Paul during one of the latter's known imprisonments, either in Rome or Cæsarea. On the other hand, it seems unlikely that Onesimus had the means to do the long journey from Colossæ to Rome or Cæsarea. It seems much more likely that he met the imprisoned Paul in Ephesus, which he could reach on foot in a few days.

Now the ' Acts of the Apostles ' say nothing about an imprisonment in Ephesus. That, however, means little. The Acts do not mention several even more important happenings in the life of St. Paul, as can be seen from 2 Corinthians ii. From the famous letter of the Roman Bishop Clemence to the Corinthians, dated A.D. 96, we know that St. Paul was imprisoned no less than seven times.

According to 1 Corinthians xv. 32, St. Paul had to fight wild beasts in the Circus in Ephesus. He will most certainly have been imprisoned on that occasion.

It is far more probable, judging by its contents, that it was an encyclical epistle, addressed to several churches, probably in Asia Minor. Now St. Paul, in his epistle to the Colossians (iv. 16) mentions a letter which he had sent to Laodicea, and which the Colossians should request to be allowed to read. The encyclical epistle which, according to this, was to be read in Laodicea, then in Ephesus and then in other communities of Asia Minor, seems to be no other than the one that we call to-day the epistle to the Ephesians.

One last example: In John v. we find the well-known moving story of the healing at the pool of Bethesda. At the edge of the pool lay many sick, blind, lame, withered. Thither one day came Jesus. He saw there a man who had been infirm for thirty-eight years. A deep compassion seized Him and he healed the man. In our New Testament, right at the beginning, we read the words: Here ' lay a great multitude of impotent folk '— ' waiting for the moving of the water. For an angel went down at a certain season into the pool and troubled the water: whosoever then first after the troubling of the water stepped in, was made whole of whatsoever disease he had.'—St. John never wrote these words. They are not contained in the oldest manuscripts, the *Sinaiticus*, the *Alexandrinus* in London (*a*), the *Vaticanus* in

Rome (*b*), and the palimpsest in Paris (*c*). From this it is clearly evident that the church of the fourth century did not know these words, and that they are therefore an addition made after the fourth century. Who made this addition? A copyist more than four hundred years after the healing at the pool of Bethesda, far from Palestine and unacquainted with the locality in Jerusalem, wondered why there were so many sick at the pool of Bethesda, and explained it to himself that an angel came down and, moving the water, gave it healing power. To make the matter understandable to his reader, he put this thought into the text, not thinking that he was thereby falsifying the original, even with the best intention. And so Christianity for many centuries looked upon these words as apostolic: only in the nineteenth century the rediscovery of the oldest manuscripts brought the fact to light that St. John himself had not written one word about the moving of the water in his gospel.

There are other passages also which, in their particular place are of purely technical significance, but do not in the least affect the faith of the Christian community. By far the greater number of differences, one can almost say all of them, are of an essentially linguistic nature, and have importance only for scientists. After all these

H

intensive researches the Bible reader can depend on it that he has the genuine writings of the apostles in his hands.

Since the sixteenth century we possess printed Greek New Testaments. But these also show many disparities, because they adhered now to one only, now to several manuscripts, and often edited by men who understood little about the matter. It is only in modern times that the fundamental principle has been established that the text of the Bible must be so respected and revered by us that we must spare no pains to get rid of the faults of the copyists. This can only be done by giving the older copies precedence over the younger. Before the discovery of the Sinai Manuscript Tischendorf had published seven editions of the Greek New Testament in more than twenty thousand copies, which he had edited according to this principle. He had thereby not lost sight of even the smallest disparities. For he was of the opinion that in the New Testament, this crown jewel of all the books of the world, nothing is indifferent, not even linguistic terms and forms. His object was to reproduce the New Testament as nearly as possible in the same state as it left the hands of the apostles.

From all this the reader can judge for himself of

what incomparable importance the *Codex Sinaiticus* is for the science of the New Testament and for the whole Church. For it is not only older than the hitherto oldest manuscript, the *Vaticanus*, which, however, at that time had not yet been made available for publication by the Pope, but also the only complete one amongst the three most important manuscripts, the *Vaticanus*, the *Alexandrinus* in London, and the Paris palimpsest of Ephraim the Syrian. All the German and other European translations of the New Testament are based on the Greek text in use since the time of Erasmus and his contemporary, Luther. This text was taken in the sixteenth century from newer Greek manuscripts, but was the same which in the Byzantine State Church during several centuries, had gone through the hands of hundreds of copyists and had been spoiled by innumerable errors. With the discovery of the *Sinaiticus* a new era has begun in this sphere. It is now possible at least to reconstruct the original apostolic text which was so widely distributed in the second century (at the time of the *Itala*) and by means of which we actually come very close to the apostolic age.

The *Codex Sinaiticus* was of the greatest importance, not only for the reconstruction of the original wording, but also for the so much disputed question of Tischendorf's time as to the genuineness of the gospels. I will only quote one small instance, which will also be clear to the layman: In the epistle of Barnabas, written about the year 120, we find the following: 'Let us beware lest, as is written, we be found among the many called but few chosen.' At first sight we do not realize how important this passage is. From whence do we know this passage? In the writings of which evangelist do we find it? Only in St. Matthew, and then only twice, in Chapters 20 and 22. What can we conclude from this? That the Gospel of St. Matthew was already known and universally acknowledged in the year 120 by the whole church as an apostolic writing. Whom have we to thank for this information? Only the *Sinaiticus*, through which the long lost epistle of Barnabas was again brought to light. It is true that this passage of the epistle of Barnabas was already known before the discovery of the Sinai Manuscript, in a very incomplete, defective, and faulty Latin translation. But this translation was considered very unreliable. Shortly before the discovery of the *Sinaiticus*, Dr. Credner, one of the greatest critics of his time, had written: 'The part of the epistle of Barnabas which contains the questionable passage no longer exists in the original Greek text, but only in an old Latin translation. It was easy for the translator to add the well-known formula: "as it is written" to the other words. For technical reasons we must therefore doubt the correctness of the text until the contrary has been proved to us.' Well, the proof came. After having lain for many centuries in the Arabian desert, among the old parchment books of the Monastery of St. Catharine, the long lost epistle of Barnabas, to the great surprise of the critics, came to light again in the original Greek language. And there on the old parchment was the disputed phrase: 'as is written'. Therefore Barnabas himself, and not his translator, had already referred to the Gospel of St. Matthew.

This was a proof that not only St. Matthew had been recognized as Holy Scripture by the young Church before A.D. 120 but the other gospels likewise, for everything points to the fact that in those days the four gospels, and not just the one or the other, were in regular church use. Especially the Gospel of St. John is often quoted beside the other three. In the writings of even the earliest Christian authors of the second century we find the four gospels taken collectively as a whole. As early as the latter half of the second century 'harmonious' works on the four gospels were undertaken, that is to say, an interlacing of the

reports of all four books, so that the different
characteristics of the four were blended into one
uniform picture.   Already Irenaeus, who died in
the year 202, compared the four gospels to the
four points of the compass.   Everything induces
one to assume that the joining together of the
four gospels into one book was undertaken as
early as the end of the first century.   At that time
the aged apostle St. John, the last of the holy men
who had personally known the Lord, had died.
This caused the writings which had been left by
the apostles to be looked upon as precious and
imperishable legacies, as authentic testimonies of
the life and teaching of the Saviour, and became
the guiding principle of faith and conduct.
Through the finding of the *Codex Sinaiticus* we
have, besides other arguments, a further proof
that the gospels, as well as the epistles, all of
which, however, were not considered authentic,
were acknowledged as Holy Scripture by the
Christian Churches before the year 120.

One last point: As already mentioned, the text
of the *Codex Sinaiticus*, in contrast to all other
known ancient Greek handwritings, has the
greatest resemblance and relationship to the
oldest Latin translation, the *Itala* of the second
century.   It therefore follows that our gospels
had up to this early time already passed through

various stages of development in their wording. If this be true, then the gospels must surely have already been in use before the close of the first century. Herewith the history of the New Testament text closely approaches the apostolic age itself. The attempts made in Tischendorf's time to represent the New Testament as being an inferior work of a later date, were thus once and for all refuted.

The discovery of this oldest manuscript of the New Testament was therefore a find that was of incalculable importance for the whole of Christianity. And only a man with the energy, perseverance, skill and expert knowledge of Tischendorf was capable of acquiring this manuscript, publishing it in the most extensive and worthy manner, and of utilizing it for the scientific research of the New Testament.

11

CONCLUSION

IF Tischendorf had done nothing more than discover, publish, and scientifically edit the *Codex Sinaiticus*, one would mention his name with the greatest appreciation in connection with the history and science of the New Testament. Right to the end of his scientific career, Tischendorf adhered with untiring industry to his great purpose, that of giving back to the Church, as far as was humanly possible, the original text of the New Testament, or at least in the form known to the early Church in the time of Irenaeus (deceased 202).

This same purpose had inspired other learned men before him, Bengel, Wetstein, Bentley, Lachmann, and others. But what these had commenced with somewhat inadequate means, Tischendorf all but brought to perfection, and far surpassed the work of his predecessors.

Towards the end of his life he wanted to embody the result of his life's work in one conclusive scientific book, the eighth edition of his larger Greek New Testament, the *Editio Octava Critica Major* (1864 to 1872), which was intended for the scientists. In this he meant to leave to the world the sum total of his analytical researches. He finished the editing of the text. The very important explanations, the Prolegomena, belonging to this, however, he unfortunately had to leave to a later hand. His Greek New Testament, intended for general use, appeared in twenty-two editions, and is distributed all over the world in many thousands. One need only compare the last edition with the first one, which in his younger days, in 1842, had brought him the dignity of the title of ' Doktor ' at the University of Breslau, to realize what immense progress had been made under his hands in thirty years.

The danger which besets most talented people, whose whole strength is given to one special branch of human knowledge, is that they may become one-sided, or even limited. Tischendorf was saved from this by his vitality of mind, without which he could never have reached his goal. He could not undertake his travels of research both in the West and the East, without the support of Governments and the promoters of science. The numerous and expensive printed editions of the oldest manuscripts could not have been made without the help of wealthy patrons. With his unusual personality and his charming manner he knew how to set about this. The two books in which he fascinatingly describes his journeys in the East are the best proof that he did not only travel as a scholar but as a man of considerable versatility. It was only a man of many interests who could have moved, as he did, amongst the aristocracy, the circles of higher science, and even feel at home at the courts of Europe who lavished on him many signs of appreciation. The King of Saxony made him Privy Councillor. The Emperor of Russia invested him and his family with a hereditary title. In both worlds his name was the best known of all the theologians of his time. The honours of all kinds bestowed on him were many. But he did not barter for these honours by sacrificing truth, nor for the sake of men did he ever renounce his Lord, nor refrain from testifying. Without fear or reticence he always acknowledged Him, and wherever it became necessary to remain firm in a difficult position, he always stood the test.

These honours pleased him, but they were only of secondary importance to him. The promotion of the science of theology and the good of the Christian community were first and foremost in his life. It was his deepest desire that his life's work might be to the glory of God and His Holy

Word. In the service of the Bible nothing was too much trouble, for to him this Book was the Word of God, and to him also the Christian faith was a matter of heart and life. He was not ashamed of the Gospel of Jesus Christ. To this service of the Kingdom of God, one may say, he dedicated his life. Proof of this is to be found also in his popular writings, which in those days were much read and translated into nearly all the European languages. One appeared under the title of *Why were our Gospels Written?* and another *Have we got the Genuine Writings of the Apostles?* In the first he set his face against the modern unbeliever, who was then appearing under the banner of science, and in the second he justified and defended science even before the Church, and upheld its freedom and right to critical analysis of the Bible text.

If we glance at the colossal number of books and publications, as well as his immense achievement in the field of text criticism and scientific research, we are astounded. According to my own calculation they number no less than seventy-two and amongst them are large collective works, such as his *Library of Original Christian Documents*, the seven volumes of his *Monumenta Sacra,* and the many editions of the Greek New Testament, into each of which went a great deal of work. He was a man of an energy and perseverance such as few people possess. His life, during which he literally rushed from one undertaking to another, was one of an exceptional volume of work.

But he still had not done enough. Great plans occupied his mind. In the spring of 1873 he wanted once more to go out to the East, and in the summer he intended going to New York to attend a large gathering of evangelical men, who had urgently invited him. But the work with which he was overburdened this spring, was more than man could cope with. This man, whose health seemed indestructible, and whose capacity for work seemed limitless, finally succumbed to the strain of overwork, which so many huge demands had from the beginning imposed upon him.

Suddenly, on May 5, 1873, in the midst of undiminished, happy work, he had a stroke, from which he could not recover. Difficult weeks and months followed. Like a child he had to learn to speak and walk again, and his daughter still remembers with emotion how hard and patiently he tried to learn to write with his left hand. But there was no change for the better. May 5 of the following year came without there being any noticeable improvement. Even a stay of several weeks in Bad Teplitz brought no change. Thus

God took his busy pen out of his hand and led him into quietness.

But just during this sorrowful time, when the world in which he had moved for so long and so successfully had ceased to exist for him, the bright childlike faith of his soul transcended all else. In unshakable faith he held fast to the grace and mercy of his Saviour. At short intervals he had one stroke after another. Finally he lapsed into unconsciousness. But during the rare intervals when the darkness lifted, the joy of his soul shone out like a reflection of the glory to come. Devoutly believing in his Lord and Saviour he died on December 7, 1874, nearly sixty years of age.

In his will are these words: ' God gave me a happy life, made beautiful by His rich blessing. It has been full of effort and toil, but the Truth was precious to me. May God bless that too, which I leave to the world: it is His work. Even though in weakness, my hand has served only Him according to my conscience and my knowledge. In science I have aimed above all things at truth. I have bowed to truth throughout. I have never formed my opinion by the applause on my right and my left. To the faithful God, whose grace has been so great, I wholeheartedly commend my family. May my much loved, faithful wife all her life retain her pure evangelical faith.   To my good and dear children I say from my heart: Be about the work of your lives with honesty and industry: seek your true salvation only in the firm belief in the Saviour.   Trust for ever and ever in the Lord.   Serve the Lord always with holy joy, solemnly and truthfully.'

By his grave stood his widow with three sons and four daughters.   The funeral sermon was preached by the well-known Pastor Ahlfeld of St. Nikolei.   To him, looking back over Tischendorf's life, it was Mount Sinai that mainly stood out.   There Moses had once seen the glory of God.   And at its foot Tischendorf too had experienced something of God's glory, when His mercy had crowned his untiring search for the oldest New Testament, with undreamed-of success.   Pastor Ahlfeld therefore chose his text from Exodus xxxiii. 20-23: ' And he said, Thou canst not see my face: for there shall no man see me, and live.   And the Lord said, Behold, there is a place by me, and thou shalt stand upon a rock: And it shall come to pass while my glory passeth by, that I will put thee in a clift of the rock, and will cover thee with my hand while I pass by: And I will take away mine hand, and thou shalt see my back parts: but my face shall not be seen.'

We, too, now see the passing by of the Lord,

who directed Tischendorf's life so wonderfully, led him by strange paths into that place between the rocks of Mount Sinai, where came to pass the greatest hour of his life; and who remained with him to the end. Of Tischendorf can be said: ' He was a burning and shining light,' as the Lord once said of a Greater One.

.   .   .   .   .

In spite of the fact that at first I had no desire to comply with the urgent request of the Bavarian Pastor's widow, to tell abroad the story of Tischendorf's life, yet while I wrote I realized over and over again: How very much worth while it was to save these things from being forgotten. It would have been a thousand pities if the story of God's strange and wonderful guidance in the search for the ancient manuscript had disappeared from the memory of our time.

And now, farewell, dear reader! It would please me if I thought that in reading, you felt as I do.

POSTSCRIPTUM

Extract from The Times *of December* 21, 1933

FAMOUS BIBLE MANUSCRIPT

The Prime Minister announced at question time in the House of Commons yesterday that the Trustees of the British Museum had decided, with the approval of the Government, to buy for £100,000 from the Soviet Government the *Codex Sinaiticus*, a famous manuscript of the Bible, which was formerly owned by the Tsar of Russia.

Printed in Great Britain by the KEMP HALL PRESS LTD.
in the City of Oxford